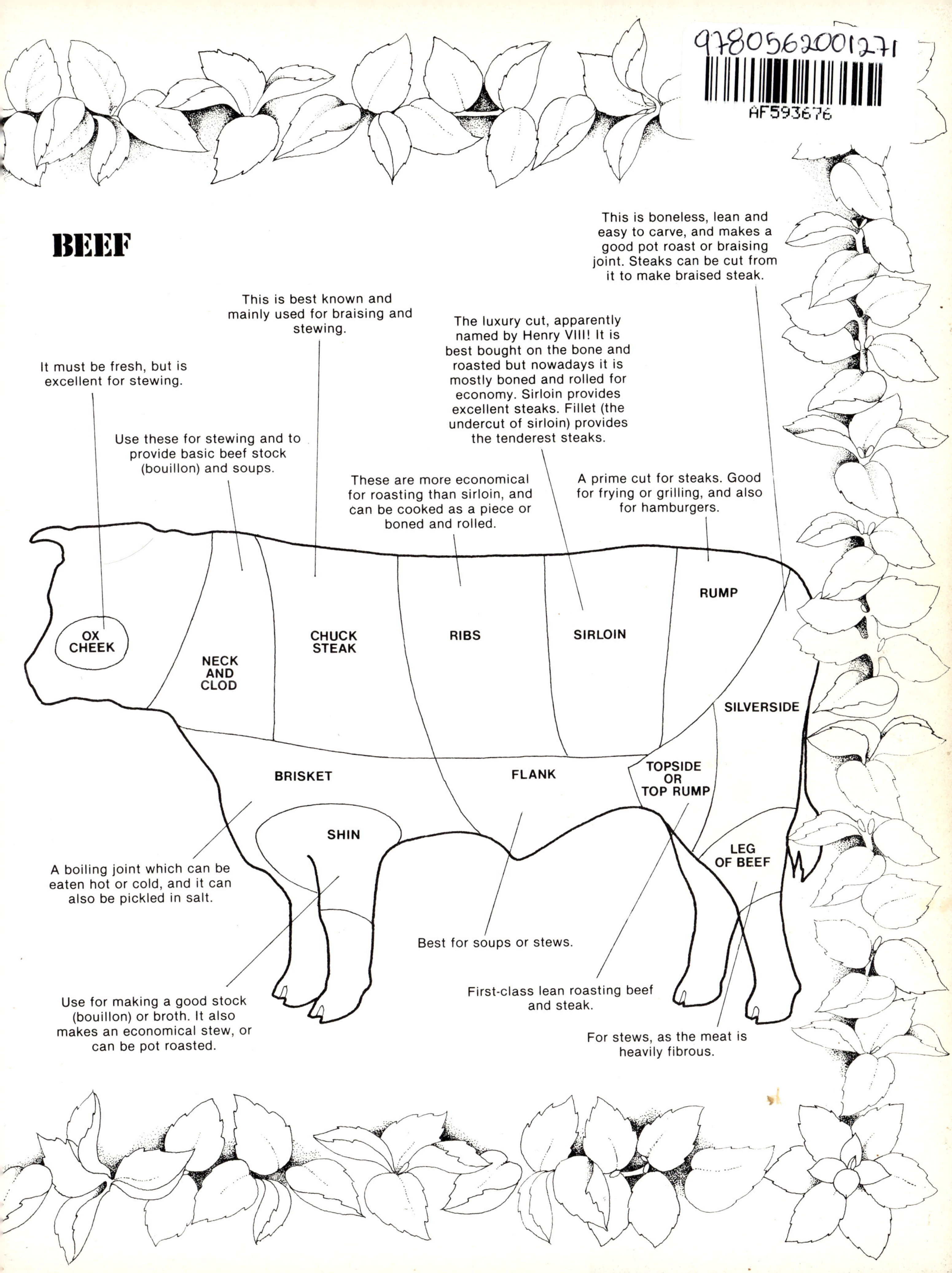
9780562001271
AF593676
BEEF
This is boneless, lean and easy to carve, and makes a good pot roast or braising joint. Steaks can be cut from it to make braised steak.
This is best known and mainly used for braising and stewing.
The luxury cut, apparently named by Henry VIII! It is best bought on the bone and roasted but nowadays it is mostly boned and rolled for economy. Sirloin provides excellent steaks. Fillet (the undercut of sirloin) provides the tenderest steaks.
It must be fresh, but is excellent for stewing.
Use these for stewing and to provide basic beef stock (bouillon) and soups.
These are more economical for roasting than sirloin, and can be cooked as a piece or boned and rolled.
A prime cut for steaks. Good for frying or grilling, and also for hamburgers.
RUMP
OX CHEEK
CHUCK STEAK
RIBS
SIRLOIN
NECK AND CLOD
SILVERSIDE
TOPSIDE OR TOP RUMP
BRISKET
FLANK
SHIN
LEG OF BEEF
A boiling joint which can be eaten hot or cold, and it can also be pickled in salt.
Best for soups or stews.
First-class lean roasting beef and steak.
Use for making a good stock (bouillon) or broth. It also makes an economical stew, or can be pot roasted.
For stews, as the meat is heavily fibrous.

MR COOK

COOKERY GUIDE FOR MEN

MR COOK

COOKERY GUIDE FOR MEN

BRIAN BINNS

Acknowledgements
Cover photograph: Terry Pickering
Colour Precision Studios, Chichester
Photography: Terry Pickering
Illustrations: Jerry Logan
Kitchen equipment and materials
for photography kindly supplied by
Snips of Chichester; Poggenpohl U.K.;
Michael Hughes Kitchen Centre, Southport;
Wedgwood; Allied Bakeries; McCormick's Spices
and *Nelson Jams*

The Author would like to thank Peter Robson for his assistance
in compiling the articles in this book.

First published in 1980 by
Sampson Low, Berkshire House,
Queen Street, Maidenhead,
Berkshire SL6 1NF

SBN 562 00127 1

Designed and produced by Autumn Publishing Ltd,
10 Eastgate Square, Chichester, Sussex PO19 1JH
Filmset in Compugraphic Helvetica by Angus Graham Associates Ltd.,
Reading, Berkshire. Printed and bound in Italy by Poligrafici Calderara.

CONTENTS

INTRODUCTION

There are cookery books for gourmets, cordon bleu cooks, vegetarians, slimmers, housewives and almost everybody else. What makes this one different is simply that it is a cookery book for men.

I have never accepted the old adage that 'a woman's place is in the kitchen', because there is room there for men too, and I do not mean just to tackle the washing up! Don't forget that most of the world's eminent chefs are men. I have suspected for a long time that the women's liberation movement started in the kitchens during the Victorian era. Our great-grandfathers were dominating the world, so our great-grandmothers turned their kitchens into a 'no-man's land'. They elevated Mrs Beeton to her rôle as a paragon of culinary virtues; and staffed their kitchens with cooks and kitchen maids who zealously guarded their downstairs domains, while the butlers retreated to their pantries.

Seriously though, most people I know appreciate good food: but I have met a great many men *and* women who claim that they do not have time to be interested in cooking very adventurous or ambitious recipes. However, I am convinced that the extra effort required in the preparation and presentation of good food can be extremely rewarding and by no means as difficult as is often imagined.

The aim behind *Mr Cook* is to give a well-balanced cookery guide for men and, to this end, the book is deliberately planned along the lines of a do-it-yourself manual. If you think of cooking along do-it-yourself lines, have the right tools and equipment to hand and follow the instructions carefully, then preparing meals can be just as satisfying as pottering about in the garden, tinkering with your car, or making your own wines or beer.

Before you even crack an egg, or peel a potato, your first task with every recipe is to get together all the tools required for each particular dish. And a special feature of this book is that at the beginning of every recipe I have listed all the hardware you will need. I also realise that every cook, no matter how new to the kitchen, will very quickly become ambitious. Thus I have not only provided a selection of simple basic recipes, but also some fairly complicated dishes. *Mr Cook* starts by whetting your appetite with *Starters, Snacks and Titbits,* and progresses through *The Humble Potato* to *Heavenly Hamburgers.* After this no holds are barred and you will find yourself getting to grips with casseroles and curries, pasta and pizza, pies and puddings, desserts, cakes and pastries...

Do remember that a cookery book is meant to be read as well as used as a guide and that there are no short cuts to success, so please follow the recipe instructions to the letter. Metric, Imperial and American equivalent measurements are given, so remember when preparing a recipe to follow only *one* set of measures. In other words if you start using metric, stick to it. Measures of teaspoons and tablespoons given in the ingredients are level, unless stated to be otherwise.

Bon appetite!

TOOLS OF THE TRADE

Do you remember the scene in Jack Lemmon's movie *The Apartment* when he tried straining cooked spaghetti through an old tennis racquet? Of course, it wasn't surprising that the meal turned into a disaster in more ways than one, because cookery is like everything else — you must use the proper tools for the job.

Before tackling any of the recipes in this, or any other book, start by taking an inventory of all the cooking utensils in your kitchen. At the very least, I think it is essential to make certain that you have the following:

A wooden spoon, a wire whisk, a grater (with sections for vegetables, as well as cheese and rind), large, medium-sized and small cook's knives, a carving knife and fork, a sharpener (not to be used on serrated knives), a serrated knife, a vegetable knife, a vegetable masher, a peeler and corer, spatulas, wooden and slotted, a soup ladle, a fish slice, a metal tablespoon, a metal slotted spoon, a large fork, a can opener, a corkscrew, pastry cutters, a pastry brush, patty tins, a piping bag, kitchen scissors, kitchen scales and a timer. Take my advice on timers (if your cooker does not have one), get one of those that can be wound up for several hours if necessary: then, if you become involved in something like a televised golf tournament, you won't forget that there is something cooking in the oven.

Check up on your stock of pots and pans and cooking vessels, too. As a minimum you will need a smallish saucepan with a lip for pouring, three saucepans with lids (two medium-sized and one large), a large frying pan (skillet) with a lid, (never use a plate to cover a frying pan; it is not only a clumsy thing to do, but it can also be dangerous if the contents flare up, and the plate can crack).

Every cook needs at least one sizeable casserole with a tight-fitting lid, but do remember that not every casserole is flameproof as well as ovenproof. I will always remember one cook (who will remain anonymous), who absent-mindedly placed an ovenproof casserole on a hot-plate which was still switched on. The result was a cracked casserole dish and 'art deco' dripping down the side of the cooker.

You will also need a pastry board, a chopping board, a rolling pin, a measuring jug, a roasting tin, a baking sheet, a mincing machine (to the uninitiated there is a bewildering choice of these particular gadgets, but start with one for raw food, which will also be able to tackle cooked food), a soup tureen and baking trays,

Top left to right:
Carving knife and fork
Cook's knives
Wooden spoons
Spatula
Kitchen scissors
Perforated ladle
Cheese grater
Slotted spoon
Piping bag
Pastry cutters
Corkscrew
Measuring jug
Slotted spatula
Rolling pin
Pastry brush
Can opener
Wire whisk
Potato peeler

Top left to right:
Mincer
Mixing bowl
Kitchen scales
Sieve
Chopping board
Saucepan
Casserole

(take care to dry these thoroughly after use to prevent rust forming, or invest in the type which are specially coated to prevent rusting, even though they are more expensive).

It certainly pays to buy the best quality utensils you can afford. This is especially true of saucepans, because although good saucepans are expensive they can last for years and save on fuel. Heavy aluminium saucepans are not really recommended although those for use with electric cookers have specially cast bases. Copper-bottomed pans heat very quickly, so that you can turn down the power, again saving fuel. If you like the easy-to-clean Teflon-coated saucepans, then take care that you follow the manufacturers' instructions about use and cleaning. Always use a wooden spoon, or wooden pot-stick, for stirring to prevent damaging the special surface. Any saucepans you buy should have insulated handles and lid knobs. And make sure that there are few corners or crevices, where dirt and grease can stick.

Every kitchen should be well ventilated with an air extractor fan to prevent it steaming up. Shelves for storing utensils should be within easy reach of everybody. Although knives should be out of the reach of children, I've seen some kitchens where the shelves have been placed so high on the walls even Rudolph Nureyev could not have leapt up and reached them with ease.

Much of the fun of cooking these days comes from using the time-saving gadgets which are available to make many of the more tedious chores seem like fun. One of the most useful is a liquidiser (blender) which has become to cookery what automatic transmission has become to motoring. It is possible to buy an expensive one which will beat, blend, chop, grate, grind and sieve. It can make batters (doughs) for Yorkshire puddings and pancakes, cream together fat, sugar and eggs for cake making; blend smoothly together the ingredients for sauces and soups; and chop herbs, onions, nuts, peel, bread and cheese. However, even a basic liquidiser will make amazing savings to your time and energy when making dishes like pâtés and soups.

Pressure cookers and slow cookers are also becoming more widely used, because of their fuel-saving qualities and the similar jobs they can do in different ways. Switch on a slow cooker in the morning, before going to work, and you return home to a perfectly prepared meal which has used very little fuel. A pressure cooker on the other hand can prepare an entire meal for three or four people in less than half the normal time. It also uses far less fuel than orthodox cooking methods.

I hope now you are ready to tackle the recipes in the following pages, and you will find cookery can be fun as well as appetizing. And, come to think about it, if this book had been around when Jack Lemmon starred in *The Apartment,* he might have been allowed to get to grips more quickly with the nubile Shirley McLaine!

Music may well be the food of love, but I believe that the art of gentle seduction comes more naturally to the man who has first successfully wined and dined his lady.

Now, that *is* food for thought, isn't it?

ORGANIZING THE MEAL

Take one well-balanced menu, add some careful preparation, stir in a measure of self-confidence, plus a dash of commonsense, and you have the real recipe for a highly successful meal.

Cooking is, without doubt, such a noble art that I am constantly surprised to find that so many men still believe that there is something almost effeminate about being spotted in the kitchen. Give a successful dinner party which you have prepared all by yourself and you race well ahead in the one-upmanship stakes. The male guests study your wife, as she plays the graceful hostess, wondering how on Earth she managed to seduce you into taking over the kitchen. Their wives gaze lingeringly at you, over their *Cannelloni,* seeing you in an entirely new light. But a word of warning...when preparing for occasions like these, take care to tackle the dishes you can make successfully and serve with aplomb. More than one meal has fallen flat because the cook's ego rose to greater heights than his soufflé!

Organizing any meal depends on the foodstuffs available, the cooking facilities and your experience as a cook. Get to know as much as you can about buying food by browsing around grocery shops and delicatessens, just as you do in bookshops and sports' goods suppliers; drop in at the local butcher's shop from time to time for a chat. It always pays to cultivate your tradesmen socially whether it be at the golf club, or in your local pub. The old pals' act works wonders and they usually *do* know what they are talking about. You can learn, too, by actually *tasting* food served to you in restaurants and elsewhere.

The most important stage in any well-planned and balanced meal is preparing the menu well in advance, having first of all tried to ascertain guests' particular tastes in food. Often I have spent weeks planning for just one dinner party, finding inspiration in the strangest of places. I have yet to discover the reason for any association of ideas, but do not be surprised if you decide on something like *Marmalade Roast Pork,* when you are cleaning the car: or — Eureka! — *My Moussaka* flashes across your mind during an important conference at work. That is often the way it happens.

The simplest approach to planning a menu is to make up your mind first about the main course, then plan the others around it. The rules are not inflexible, but basically I think that prominent ingredients, methods of cooking, colours and textures should not be repeated in different courses in the same meal. When you

have decided upon your menu, read through the recipes carefully and make certain that you understand all that is required. Then check through your hardware (pots, pans, serving dishes) to make sure that you have enough for the occasion. Too few of these can be as disastrous as having too many cooks, because no matter how superbly cooked the meal, the host who serves his guests with creamed potatoes from the saucepan is probably best regarded as eccentric.

It is important to make out a list of all the ingredients needed beforehand. This list must include the obvious items such as salt, pepper, cooking, oil and flour. Also make certain that you have enough of everything as you cannot substitute any of these basics at the last minute.

Prepare as much of the meal as you can in advance. If you are making a pâté, for example, it can be made the day before and stored in the refrigerator. But do remember to take it out of the fridge at least one hour before you expect to serve it. Apart from enhancing the flavour, this saves wear and tear on knives, teeth and tempers. Make a rough workplan, so you don't forget anything, such as removing food from the freezer.

Always take care when working in the kitchen. One of the things I have always admired about women is that they appear to have an instinctive sixth sense for safety. They can bustle about among the pots and pans, cookers, cats and kids, coping with half-a-dozen chores, seemingly all at once. Yet rarely do they appear to put a foot (or elbow) in the wrong place. So a workman-like approach is the most successful and the safest of all. That means having as much clear space to work in as possible. Therefore, when making the meal, it is advisable to clear up, wash up and stack away everything that is no longer needed as soon as possible.

Give yourself lots of elbow room and TIME to organize your cooking activities as methodically as you do your everyday working activities.

With dinner parties in particular, it is very important to make quite certain before starting to plan the meal that you have all the tableware, glassware and cutlery you need to cater for that particular occasion. Some people might consider it rather chic to throw a dinner party serving fish and chips wrapped in newspaper, with individual finger-bowls, but you can't really tackle smoked trout without the right cutlery. And remember little points such as keeping near the table, such things as a cork screw, serving spoons, spare napkins, mats for very hot dishes...

A suitable table setting also adds a great deal to the pleasure of a good meal, and the way in which it is presented is as much a matter of individual choice as the menu itself. Some people prefer some kind of colourful setting with tablecloths; others prefer tablemats. If you like a centre piece with a flower arrangement, then do make sure that the arrangement is a low-lying one. Apart from the fact that a good host likes to keep a watchful eye on everybody else's plate, he can claim a certain *droit de seigneur* by making sure that the most attractive women present sits facing him. And he should be able to enjoy the view.

Of course, the best-laid plans of mice and male cooks, can go awry. Sometimes your meal might not turn out quite as well as expected. But don't despair! Just open the kitchen window to let the fumes escape, provide another bottle of whisky for your guests, then make your excuse about having to move the car and leave...hot-foot for the nearest take-away!

CREAM OF ONION SOUP WITH WHITE WINE

Hardware

chopping board
cook's medium-sized knife
small knife
wooden spoon
2.25 litres/4 pints (10 cups) saucepan
frying or sauté pan (skillet)
liquidiser (blender)

Ingredients (serves 4—6)

4 medium-sized onions
50g/2 ozs (2 ozs) butter
approx. 150ml/¼ pint (⅔ cup) dry white wine
300ml/½ pint (1¼ cups) milk
900ml/1½ pints (3¾ cups) chicken stock (bouillon)
2 × 5ml spoons/2 teaspoons (2 teaspoons) white flour
salt and white pepper to taste
150ml/¼ pint (⅔ cup) single cream (light cream)

Method

1 Roughly chop 3 of the onions and cook them gently in half the butter in a saucepan until they are soft. Do not let them get brown.

2 Sprinkle on the flour and blend it in. Continue to cook, stirring all the time for 2 or 3 minutes.

3 Add the wine and then the milk gradually, followed by the stock, stirring continuously. Simmer the soup gently for 40 minutes.

4 Whilst it is cooking, slice the remaining onion finely into roundels. Cook gently in the rest of the butter in the frying pan for 4 or 5 minutes leaving them slightly crisp. Place on one side.

5 When the soup is cooked, liquidise it. Pour it back into the saucepan. Adjust the seasoning, stir in the cream and then the onion rings. Return to the boil and serve.

Chef's Hints

This soup should not be too thick. The glass of wine gives an interesting sharp flavour, but can be left out if you prefer a more bland taste. The onion rings create an attractive garnish and some crispy fried cubes of bread give added interest.

CREAM OF JERUSALEM ARTICHOKE SOUP

Hardware

2 large saucepans
small knife
liquidiser (blender)

Ingredients (serves 4)

450g/1 lb (1 lb) Jerusalem artichokes
1.15 litres/2 pints (5 cups) chicken stock (bouillon)
300ml/½ pint (1¼ cups) single cream (light cream)
chopped parsley or chives for garnish
1 × 5ml/teaspoon (1 teaspoon) salt
salt and white pepper to taste

Method

1 Wash the artichokes. Put them in a saucepan, and cover them with cold water. Add a teaspoon of salt, bring to the boil and cook for 5 minutes.

2 Drain the water from the artichokes and as soon as they are cool enough to handle, remove the skins. As they are very 'knobbly' this is not the easiest job and is best done with a small pointed knife and plenty of patience.

3 Put the peeled artichokes into a saucepan containing the stock and bring to the boil. Cook gently for 15 minutes, then allow to cool sufficiently to put into a liquidiser.

4 Liquidise a little at a time. Return the mixture to the saucepan, season with salt and white pepper. (This is a white soup therefore I dislike specks of black pepper in it). Add the cream and reheat gently. Adjust the seasoning if necessary, garnish and serve.

Chef's Hints

Replace the artichokes with a similar weight of celeriac. Simply remove the thick skin and then cut the celeriac into small chunks, treating it then like a peeled artichoke. This also makes a delicious soup.

Carrot soup served with cream and crusty brown bread.

CARROT SOUP

This soup is seldom made, but it is so easy and so good that everyone should try it. It is an attractive looking soup and delicious to eat.

Hardware

2.25 litres/4 pints (10 cups) saucepan
cook's medium-sized knife
cheese grater
wooden spoon
large bowl
liquidiser (blender) or sieve

Ingredients (serves 4)

450g/1 lb (1 lb) carrots
1 medium-sized onion
grated rind of ½ orange
50g/2 ozs (2 ozs) butter
1.15 litres/2 pints (5 cups) chicken stock (bouillon)
sugar to taste
salt and freshly ground pepper to taste

Method

1 Grate the carrots coarsely, and roughly chop the onions.

2 Melt the butter in a saucepan. Add the carrots, onions and grated orange rind, and cook gently for 15 minutes. This is best accomplished by stirring over a medium heat until all the ingredients are coated with butter and very hot. Put on the pan lid, turn the heat very low and cook until tender, shaking the pan occasionally to prevent sticking.

3 Add the chicken stock and simmer for 1 hour, then liquidise or press through a sieve.

4 Season to taste, bring to the boil and serve.

Chef's Hints

Crispy fried bread cubes are excellent to serve with this soup, and as a touch of luxury, add a teaspoon of whipped cream to each portion (I like sour cream with lemon juice).

TOMATO SOUP

The amount of garlic used in this soup depends very much on your taste; for me 6 large cloves would not be too much! As with any soup — the better the stock the better the soup.

Hardware

2.25 litres/4 pints (10 cups) saucepan
small sharp knife
wooden spoon
potato peeler
liquidiser (blender)

Ingredients (serves 6)

3 medium-sized onions
2 large cloves garlic
50g/2 ozs (2 ozs) butter
400g/14 ozs (14 ozs) can tomatoes
1.15 litres/2 pints (5 cups) chicken stock (bouillon)
3 medium-sized potatoes
salt and freshly ground black pepper
a good pinch thyme

Method

1 Cut the onions into thin slices and chop the garlic finely.

2 Melt the butter in a saucepan, put in the onions, thyme and garlic and stew gently for 5 minutes.

3 Chop or liquidise the tomatoes to a purée, and add them, including their juices, to the onions and garlic.

4 Peel and dice the potato, and add to the saucepan with the chicken stock. Bring the soup to the boil then simmer gently for 1¼ hours. Adjust the seasoning with salt and freshly ground black pepper.

Chef's hints

Like most soups this one can be served in a variety of ways: liquidise half the soup and mix with the unliquidised half to produce a hearty broth-type soup; liquidise all the soup and serve with a good teaspoon of sour (cultured) cream per portion; serve it as it is, with grated cheese (Parmesan or Cheddar) or with croûtons (cubes of fried bread). This is how I like it.

Magnificent Mushroom Soup

MAGNIFICENT MUSHROOM SOUP

This is a dark but interesting looking soup with a delicious, mushroomy flavour. Pour it into a heated tureen or individual soup bowls and garnish with parsley, or fresh chervil if you happen to have some.

Hardware

cook's knife and a small sharp knife
2 large saucepans
wooden spoon
sieve
large frying pan (skillet)

Ingredients (serves 4—6)

12 large flat mushrooms (small white mushrooms must not be used)
1 x 15 ml spoon/1 tablespoon (1 tablespoon) finely chopped parsley
a good pinch dried thyme
1 x 5ml spoon/1 teaspoon (1 teaspoon) dried tarragon
fresh chervil (optional)
salt and freshly ground black pepper
1.75 litres/3 pints (7½ cups) chicken stock (bouillon)
100g/4 ozs (4 ozs) butter
juice of one medium-sized lemon

Method

1 Take the stalks off the mushrooms and chop them into small pieces. Cut the caps neatly into slices across, about 5 mm/¼ inch thick. Put the slices to one side.

2 Chop the onion finely, melt half the butter in a large saucepan, add the onions, mushroom stalks and herbs, cook gently for 5 minutes, stirring occasionally.

3 Heat the stock, and add it to the mushroom and onion mixture. Season with salt and freshly ground black pepper and cook gently for 30 minutes. Strain through a fine sieve.

4 Melt some more butter 50g/2 ozs (2 ozs) in a sauté or frying pan, add the sliced mushroom caps and cook gently for 10 minutes, stirring carefully now and again, to cook evenly but without breaking the slices. Mix the lemon juice through these mushroom slices and add them, plus the liquid that will have formed, to the strained stock. Simmer gently for 10 minutes and serve.

EASY LIVER PÂTÉ

This pâté is at its best using goose livers, if you can get them. However, duck livers are also excellent; chicken livers are easy to get and very good. Do make sure the livers are fresh and that you remove all unsightly bits and pieces. It is easy to spoil your pâté with the bitter taste of the gall bladder, which lies close to the liver and creates the yellow/green discolouration — so chop it off!

Hardware

small sharp knife
large frying pan (skillet)
wooden spoon
liquidiser (blender) or sieve
pan to melt butter
earthenware dish or dishes

Ingredients (serves 4-6)

450g/1 lb (1 lb) livers of chicken, duck, goose or turkey
50g/2 ozs (2 ozs) butter for frying
50g/2 ozs (2 ozs) butter for mixing
25g/1 oz (1 oz) butter for coating
salt and freshly ground pepper
A good pinch of each of the following to make up 2 × 5 ml spoons/2 teaspoons (2 teaspoons): marjoram, nutmeg, cinnamon, ground cloves, sage
3 crushed juniper berries
a tiny pinch cayenne pepper
120ml/4 fl oz (½ cup) brandy
120ml/4 fl oz (½ cup) Madeira, sherry or port
1 large clove garlic, finely chopped

Easy Liver Pâté

Method

1 Sort through the livers and cut off any discoloured and yellow or green parts. Remove the sinews and membranes if there are any.

2 Melt the butter for frying and add the livers. Stir the livers until they are evenly coloured, then cook them on a medium heat for 2 minutes. They should still be pink in the middle.

3 (a) Put the entire contents of the frying pan into your liquidiser. Add the butter for mixing, spices, berries, seasoning and garlic. Rinse the pan out with the brandy and the wine and add that too. Liquidise in short bursts until smooth and well blended. Taste and adjust the seasoning with any of the flavourings or a little extra brandy, Madeira, sherry or port.
(b) A rougher pâté can be made by forcing the liver through a sieve, adding the other ingredients, and then mixing it by hand with a wooden spoon, instead of using a liquidiser.

4 Pour (the mixture will be just pourable) into earthenware dishes (or one large one), and spread level. Melt 25g/1 oz (1 oz) butter and cover the surface of the pâté with it. Refrigerate until an hour before required.

Left: Spooning melted butter over the pâté.

CREAMY LEEK PILLOWS

Hardware

sharp medium-sized knife
large saucepan
small mixing bowl
wooden spoon
teaspoon
pastry brush
rolling pin
baking trays

Ingredients (makes about 18—20)

450g/1 lb (1 lb) cleaned and trimmed leeks
150ml/¼ pint (⅔ cup) single cream (light cream)
salt and white pepper to taste
25g/1 oz (1 oz) white flour
150ml/¼ pint (⅔ cup) milk
25g/1 oz (1 oz) butter
450g/1 lb (1 lb) puff pastry (bought)
egg for glazing the pastry

Method

Filling

1 Cut the cleaned and trimmed leeks into 5 mm/¼ inch rounds. Place them in a saucepan with the single cream, salt and pepper. Bring to the boil, reduce the heat and simmer gently for approximately 5 minutes. This leaves the leeks quite crisp and slightly undercooked.

2 Whilst the leeks are cooking, mix the milk and flour together to a smooth pourable paste. Add this to the simmering leeks, stirring gently all the time to form a smooth thick sauce with rounds of leeks in it. Dot the butter over the surface and allow to cool.

Pillows

3 Roll out the puff pastry to a little less than 3 mm/⅛ inch in thickness and cut out 10 cm/4 inch circles. Fold the trimmings together, allow them to relax for 5 minutes, then roll out and cut more circles until the pastry is used up. You should have 18-20 circles.

4 Using your rolling pin, roll the discs lightly across the centre, forming an oval, thinner across the middle than at the edges. Arrange them neatly in rows on your work surface.

5 Dampen the edges of these ovals with water and then place a good teaspoon of leek filling in the centre of each (the more you can put in, the more delicious they will be — but remember you have to seal the edges together round the filling). Fold the pastry over the filling to form a half moon shape and seal the edges. Pressing them well together around the edges. Beat the egg a little with a fork and brush the pastry lightly with it. Place the pillows on lightly-greased baking trays and bake at 190C/375F Gas mark 5 for 15 minutes or until golden.

Chef's Hints

Sealing the pastry is important or your filling will flow out. Don't get the pastry too wet, but ensure it is damp in all the parts that have to be sealed.

Creamy Leek Pillows

GREEK BEANS

Hardware

bowl
heavy frying pan (skillet)
wooden spoon
cook's small knife
saucepan

Ingredients (serves 2)

225g/8 ozs (8 ozs) dried butter beans
50g/2 ozs (2 ozs) butter
2 × 15ml spoons/2 tablespoons (2 tablespoons) olive oil
1 medium-sized onion
2 cloves garlic
400g/14 ozs (14 ozs) canned tomatoes
salt and freshly ground pepper to taste

Method

1 Put the beans into the bowl, cover with cold water and soak overnight.

2 Drain the beans, put into the saucepan, cover with cold water and add a little salt. Bring to the boil and simmer until the beans are tender but not mushy (about 1 hour). Drain and reserve.

3 Melt the butter and the olive oil in the heavy frying pan.

4 Chop the onion and the garlic, add to the butter and cook gently until soft.

5 Roughly chop the tomatoes and add, with the juice from the can, to the onion in the pan. Season well with salt and freshly ground pepper. Mix well and cook until the juice has reduced by about a third.

6 Add the butter beans, mix gently so as not to break the skins and continue cooking until the beans are heated through.

Chef's Hints

Place in a warmed serving dish and decorate with one or two sprigs of fresh parsley. This dish can be eaten on its own as a starter, or with grilled (broiled) meat and salad.

BAKED JACKET POTATOES

I have tried numerous ways to speed up or improve the cooking of jacket potatoes, but this method always produces the fluffiest, tastiest and crispest-skinned potato of any.

Method

1 Choose large potatoes of a similar size, wash them well and remove any unsightly eyes or blemishes. Prick all over with a fork to prevent bursting and put them into the oven at 190C/375F Gas mark 5, for 1½ hours or until they are cooked. This obviously depends on the size of the potatoes and to some extent the variety.

2 When they are tender, take them from the oven, cover with a clean cloth and gently squeeze them all over, breaking the interior without breaking the skin.

3 Make a cut in the form of a cross on the top of the potato and gently press in the sides to burst it open. Sprinkle with salt, put in a good-sized knob of butter and serve.

Chef's Hints

This is the ideal potato to serve with rich casserole dishes, such as Bean and Beef Stew (p.56) and is good to serve with grilled steaks (p.48). If liked, top with one of the following: sour cream and chives; a chunk of soft buttery cheese or garlic butter.

To make garlic butter: Peel two garlic cloves and boil in a small amount of water for about four minutes. Drain the water and chop up garlic very finely. Soften 50g/2 ozs (2 ozs) of butter and then mix in the garlic. Chill thoroughly.

Baked jacket potatoes with a tasty filling are also very good as a snack: To do this, instead of cutting a cross, slice about 5mm/¼ inch of the top, scoop out most of the flesh, mash it and season it. Mix with any of the fillings below, replace into the skin and pop into a hot oven for approximately 10 minutes to re-heat.

Fillings: prawns (shrimp) and mayonnaise; Cheddar, Stilton or any tasty cheese cut into small cubes; or diced chicken breast, ham and tongue and a little butter.

Rösti With Ham

RÖSTI WITH HAM

Hardware

large saucepan
cheese grater
knife
palette knife
plate
non-stick frying pan (skillet)

Ingredients (serves 2)

675g/1½ lbs (1½ lbs) potatoes
1 large onion
50g/2 ozs (2 ozs) butter (chilled)
100g/4 ozs (4 ozs) cooked ham (boiled or roast)
50g/1 oz (1 oz) butter for frying
salt and freshly ground pepper to taste

Method

1 Peel the potatoes and boil them in salted water until three parts cooked. Allow them to cool and then grate them coarsely. *Do not overcook the potatoes.*

2 Chop the onion very finely and cut the ham and the chilled butter into 5mm/¼ inch dice.

3 Mix the potatoes, onions and butter together. Add the ham and season to taste.

4 In a large, non-stick, frying pan, melt the butter for frying and swirl it round, coating all the surface of the pan. Get it really hot but do not burn it.

5 Empty in the potato mixture and pat it into shape with a palette knife, forming a square sided cake about 25mm/1 inch thick.

6 Cook this over a gentle heat for approximately 15 minutes, adjusting the heat so that a thin but firm brown crust is formed.

7 Brush melted butter over a plate large enough to cover the frying pan. Place it butter side down on to the Rösti and carefully invert the pan so that the Rösti ends up on the plate. Slide it back into the pan to cook the other side for a further 15 minutes. Keep the Rösti in shape by gently patting it with a palette knife.

8 Using the plate method when you turned the Rösti, empty it out of the frying pan, cut it into sections and serve.

BASIC PANCAKE BATTER

The pankcake batter given for this recipe is simple and straightforward, but it makes consistently good pancakes and I use it every time I need pancakes. Many recipes include sugar, butter and flavourings — perhaps they do give a pancake a little more character — but they make it more difficult to handle and to fry. Pancakes from my simple batter are quite excellent to eat and easy to handle and cook.

Hardware

2 mixing bowls
whisk
sieve
heavy frying pan (skillet)
wooden spoon
spatula or palette knife

Ingredients (makes approx. 16 pancakes)

150g/5 ozs (5 ozs) sieved plain flour (all purpose flour)
pinch salt
2 medium-sized eggs
approx. 300ml/½ pint (1¼ cups) milk

Method

1 Sieve the flour and salt into a bowl.

2 Beat the eggs lightly and add to the flour and salt, mixing well.

3 Add the milk a little at a time, beating each time to ensure a smooth batter. The batter should be the consistency of single cream (light cream).

4 Allow the batter to stand for at least 2 hours before using.

5 Brush a 100-130 mm/4-5 inch heavy frying pan with oil and allow it to become very hot.

6 Pour in enough batter to *thinly* cover the bottom of the pan and cook over a high heat for about 1 minute. Turn and cook the other side for about 30 seconds. Turn out on to a warm dish.

7 Repeat this process until all the batter is used up. You should have at least 16 pancakes.

Roll up the filled pancakes and place them in a buttered dish.

CHICKEN AND SPINACH PANCAKES WITH CHEESE SAUCE

Filled pancakes, such as for this recipe, should be made a little thicker than basic pancakes in order to contain the filling and to create the eating quantity required in the dish. They make a fairly substantial first course.

Hardware

mixing bowl
spatula or palette knife
whisk
sieve
frying pan (skillet)
2 large saucepans
slotted spoon
wooden spoon
cheese grater
gratin dish (must also be flame-proof)

Ingredients (serves 6—8)

Filling:
675g/1½ lbs (1½ lbs) fresh spinach
350g/12 ozs (12 ozs) cooked breast of chicken
50g/2 ozs (2 ozs) butter
salt, black pepper and grated nutmeg to taste
50g/2 ozs (2 ozs) cream cheese

Cheese sauce
100g/4 ozs (4 ozs) butter
75g/3 ozs (3 ozs) plain flour (all purpose flour)
1.5 litres/2 pints (5 cups) milk
salt and white pepper to taste
225g/8 ozs (8 ozs) Double Gloucester cheese, grated

Method

Filling

1 Make the pancakes, allowing 2 per person, and keep warm.

2 Prepare the filling. Remove the largest stalks from the spinach and wash the rest well in salted water.

3 Shake and put the spinach in a saucepan; there will be sufficient water left on the spinach to cook it. Cook for about 8 minutes, then using a slotted spoon, squeeze the surplus water out of the spinach.

4 Season with salt, black pepper and grated nutmeg. Add the butter, cream cheese, and chopped chicken breast and mix together.

5 Divide the spinach and chicken mixture between the pancakes. Roll up and arrange in a buttered gratin dish, pour the cheese sauce over the pancakes and place under a very hot grill until the top is nicely browned. Serve immediately.

Cheese sauce

1 Melt the butter, add the flour and cook for 2-3 minutes over a medium heat.

2 Heat the milk nearly to boiling point and gradually add to the butter and flour mixture, stirring all the time to produce a smooth sauce. Season to taste and allow to simmer gently for 5 minutes.

3 Add the grated cheese, mix well and put to one side until ready for use. Any type of cheese can be used for this sauce. I occasionally use up left-overs from the cheese board. It is superb with Stilton.

Just before serving pour the cheese sauce over the pancakes.

COOKING BASIC VEGETABLES

English cooks have long had a reputation for overcooking and using too much water when cooking vegetables. Unfortunately, I think it is justified and not much enthusiasm is being shown towards correcting the situation.

Most vegetables are good eaten raw so it stands to reason that only minimum cooking is required in most instances. I do not believe, however, that exact times can be given as so much depends on the maturity, freshness, size, variety, and the way the vegetable is cut.

Below is a list of the most popular vegetables which I believe are at their best plainly cooked and served with a generous slice of butter. Seasoning should consist of salt, freshly ground black pepper and sugar to taste. To cook, season with salt and pour on boiling or cold water as directed.

Hard Drum Type Cabbage: shred and cook in 25mm/1 inch boiling water. Threequarters fill the pan with the cabbage; cook with the lid on for 5-7 minutes. Drain well and add a large knob of butter.

Spring Cabbage: remove very coarse ribs and tear the leaves into halves or quarters, then cook as above but for 8-10 minutes. Mix a generous portion of butter through the cabbage.

Cauliflower: trim off all outside leaves, scoop out the base of the centre stem. Place in a suitable pan, with a little salt. Pour on boiling water until it is 25mm/1 inch deep and cook with the lid on for 10-15 minutes. Timing for this vegetable is difficult and a careful watch and frequent testing is advised until you gain experience.

French Beans (Green Beans): trim or 'top and tail' and remove string that runs down most beans; don't cut them unless they are very big. Put into a saucepan, season, pour on boiling water just to cover, and cook at a slow boil for about 5 minutes. Serve with a slice of butter.

Swede (Rutabaga): a much underrated vegetable. Peel and cut it into 15mm/½ inch slices, season, cover with cold water. Cook with lid on for 10-20 minutes, drain well and mash with a potato masher or a fork, with lots of butter. Adjust the seasoning with salt, pepper and sugar. Put some energy into this and make a fairly smooth purée.

Parsnips: peel, cut off top and bottom. Cut in half lengthwise, cover with cold water, bring to the boil and cook for 5 minutes. Drain well, spread in a single layer in a roasting pan, and sprinkle liberally with fat from the roast or a mixture of butter and lard. Roast them with your meat for 20-30 minutes or until tender and golden. It helps to baste these occasionally.

Brussels Sprouts: trim off all the outer leaves and the hard base of the stem. Make a cut in the base of the stem in the form of a cross to help evenness of cooking. Season, barely cover with boiling water and simmer uncovered for 5-7 minutes.

Celery: I like to cut celery into small batons and cook them in seasoned boiling water for 5-6 minutes. Drain off the water, sprinkle with a little chopped parsley and serve with a slice of butter on top.

New Potatoes: It very much depends on the size, maturity and freshness, but unless you are finicky, don't peel them. Simply wash them well, cover with salted cold water, bring to the boil and cook until tender in a covered pan for 10-15 minutes.

Roast Potatoes: Peel old potatoes and cut into even-sized pieces. Heat some lard or dripping in a roasting pan. Put in the potatoes and spoon the fat over them, or roll them in it, to coat them evenly. Roast for 1½ hours at 180C/350F Gas mark 4. It helps to baste and turn the potatoes occasionally thereafter.

ASPARAGUS

If you don't have a deep pan, the asparagus can be cooked lying flat, half covered with boiling salted water; but take great care over timing, as the tips will cook well before the lower stalk. Alternatively, if you possess a steamer, this is an excellent method of cooking them.

Hardware

deep saucepan
cook's small knife
absorbent paper
string
napkin

Ingredients (serves 4)

900g/ 2 lbs (2 lbs) asparagus
1 × 2.5ml/½ teaspoon (½ teaspoon) salt

Method

1 Cut off the bottom 25mm/1 inch of the asparagus stalks and endeavour to bring them all to a similar length. Scrape down the lower parts of the stems to remove the thin skin.

2 Divide the stalks into bundles of 6 or 8, combining stalks of similar thickness; tie these bundles together.

3 Ideally, using a pan deep enough to hold the bundles upright, fill with water three quarters of the way up the stalks. Simmer the bundles in salted water with the lid on, until they are tender, for 10-15 minutes. Thinner stalks will cook more rapidly.

4 Carefully remove and drain them on absorbent paper. Untie the string and serve loosely wrapped in a clean napkin.

Chef's Hints

Serve the asparagus with plenty of melted, unsalted butter, or cold with a vinaigrette dressing.

Above: Ratatouille

Asparagus can be served loosely wrapped in a clean napkin.

GLAZED CARROTS

Hardware

large saucepan
vegetable peeler
cook's medium-sized knife

Ingredients (serves 2)

3 medium-sized carrots
25g/1 oz (1 oz) butter
1 × 5ml spoon/1 teaspoon (1 teaspoon) sugar
salt and freshly ground pepper to taste

Method

1 Peel the carrots and cut them into either thin sticks or slices.

2 Put the butter, salt, pepper and sugar into a saucepan, add the carrots and barely cover with water.

3 Cook over a low heat, uncovered, for 12—15 minutes. The liquid should be almost evaporated, leaving a syrupy glaze over the carrots.

RATATOUILLE

This is a dish which has become very popular and can be bought frozen in many food shops. In my opinion, however, none of them are anything like the true dish. Ratatouille is easy to make and you can make a far superior dish for half the price you would pay for the frozen version.

Hardware

cook's medium-sized knife
large frying pan (skillet) or flameproof casserole dish
wooden spoon

Ingredients (serves 6)

150ml/¼ pint (⅔ cup) olive oil
1 large onion
2 cloves garlic
100g/4 ozs (4 ozs) green or red pepper
100g/4 ozs (4 ozs) courgettes (zucchini)
175g/6 ozs (6 ozs) aubergines (eggplants)
450g/1 lb (1 lb) tomatoes
1 × 15ml spoon/1 tablespoon (1 tablespoon) finely chopped parsley
1 × 5ml spoon/1 teaspoon (1 teaspoon) ground coriander
1 × 15ml spoon/1 tablespoon (1 tablespoon) dried basil
salt and freshly ground black pepper to taste

Method

1 Heat the olive oil in a large frying pan or flameproof casserole dish.

2 Finely slice the onion and garlic, add to the oil and cook gently without browning for 4 minutes.

3 Remove the seeds from the peppers. Slice the peppers, tomatoes, courgettes and aubergines into rings. Add to the mixture in the frying pan. Stir all these ingredients together and allow to cook gently.

4 Mix in the herbs and season very lightly with salt and pepper. Bring the mixture to the boil, reduce the heat and cook very slowly, uncovered, for at least 2 hours.

5 Taste the mixture and adjust the seasoning.

CABBAGE WITH CHEESE SAUCE

Hardware

large saucepan
cook's medium-sized knife
gratin dish (flameproof)

Ingredients (serves 2)

2 good-sized heads spring cabbage
300ml/½ pint (1¼ cups) cheese sauce (p.25)

Method

1 Discard the outer leaves of the cabbage and cut out all the coarse central stalks. Wash the remaining leaves very carefully.

2 Cut the leaves into about 5mm/¼ inch strips and sprinkle with salt.

3 Put the cabbage into a large saucepan, pour on about 300ml/½ pint (1¼ cups) boiling water and cook rapidly with the lid on the pan, for 5 minutes or until tender.

4 Drain the cabbage *well,* turn it on to a chopping board and chop several times with a sharp cook's knife.

5 Put the cabbage into the bottom of the gratin dish. Cover with cheese sauce and cook in an oven at 190C/375F Gas mark 5, for 20 minutes or until the top is golden.

Chef's Hints

The above recipe is a good way of using left-over cabbage or other vegetables.

STUFFED TOMATOES

Hardware

medium-sized knife
deep frying pan (skillet)
ovenproof serving dish

Ingredients (serves 6)

1 medium-sized onion
2 x 15ml spoons/2 tablespoons (2 tablespoons) vegetable oil
1 x 5ml spoon/1 teaspoon(1 teaspoon) ground ginger, or pinch of fresh chilli pepper, finely chopped
3 x 5ml spoons/3 teaspoons (3 teaspoons) garam masala
3 x 5ml spoons/3 teaspoons (3 teaspoons) ground coriander
3 x 5ml spoons/3 teaspoons (3 teaspoons) fresh mint, chopped (optional)
salt and pepper
6 large tomatoes (firm, slightly under-ripe)
2 x 5ml spoons/2 teaspoons (2 teaspoons) sugar
100g/4 ozs (4 ozs) peas, frozen
100g/4 ozs (4 ozs) sweetcorn, frozen
100g/4 ozs (4 ozs) Cheddar cheese or similar, cut into 5mm/¼ inch dice.

Method

1 Finely chop the onion, heat the oil in the frying pan, add the onion and fry gently until it is soft.

2 Add the ginger, chilli, garam masala, coriander, mint if used, and salt and pepper. Cook for a further 2 minutes.

3 Slice the tops off the tomatoes, scoop out the middle and add it to the contents of the frying pan. Cook until most of the free liquid has evaporated.

4 Put the tomato shells upside down to drain.

5 Add the sugar, peas and corn to the mixture in the frying pan and cook for 3-4 minutes. Adjust the seasoning and mix in the diced cheese.

6 Put the tomato shells into the ovenproof serving dish and fill them with the mixture, leting the surplus overflow. Cook at 180C/350F Gas mark 4, for 15 minutes.

Serve with plain grilled meats or fish.

Courgettes With Herbs
garnished with parsley.

COURGETTES WITH HERBS

Hardware

1.15 litres/2 pints (5 cups) saucepan
large frying pan (skillet)
medium-sized knife
sieve for straining
serving dish

Ingredients (serves 4)

450g/1 lb (1 lb) courgettes (zucchini)
50g/2 ozs (2 ozs) butter
1 × 5ml spoon/1 teaspoon (1 teaspoon) fresh parsley
1 × 5ml spoon/1 teaspoon (1 teaspoon) fresh chives
1 × 5ml spoon/1 teaspoon (1 teaspoon) fresh chervil
a squeeze of lemon juice
salt and freshly ground black pepper

Method

1 Wash and 'top and tail' the courgettes .

2 Chop the herbs very finely.

3 Cut the courgettes into slices 3mm/$\frac{1}{8}$ inch thick. Place them into the saucepan and just cover with water. Bring to the boil, lower the heat and simmer for 3 minutes. Strain off the water.

4 Heat the butter in a frying pan, add the courgettes and the herbs. Season with salt and pepper and cook for a minute or so until they are very hot.

5 Squeeze the lemon juice on to them and turn into a hot serving dish.

Chef's Hints

Courgettes should still be crisp when served and the cooking time should be adjusted to achieve this — even three minutes can be too long, if the courgettes are picked freshly from your garden.

HOW TO COOK CHIPS

The best way to cook chips is to fry them in two stages: stage one is blanching and stage two is browning. The first stage cooks the potato thoroughly, and the second stage browns and crisps the outside.

Follow these simple rules and your chips will always be good.

1 The frying medium can be varied, using dripping(s), lard (shortening), ground nut (peanut) oil or olive oil. All impart their own particular flavour — olive oil to me is very special. Always make sure there is room for the chips to move around in the pan.

2 Rinse the chipped potatoes before frying and dry them as well as is practical, to prevent spluttering and to preserve the life of your oil.

3 The temperature of the oil for blanching should be 170C/325F (see below) and depending on how thick you have cut the potatoes, will take between 4 and 6 minutes. They should be soft, but only pale yellow in colour — the temperature of the fat or oil will have dropped to 160C/312F (see below).

4 Lift out the frying basket and allow the chips to drain over the pan thoroughly. Re-heat the oil to 175C/337F (see below), and plunge the basket back in to cook to a golden brown. This should take only 3 minutes. Drain the chips well in the basket and then empty them into a warmed bowl. Serve immediately.

Chef's Hints

Different fats and oils give off vapour or smoke at different temperatures, so it always pays to use a thermometer. However, if you don't want to go to the trouble of buying a special thermometer you can test the temperature by dropping a cube of day-old bread into the fat. It should rise to the surface, crispy and golden, after about a minute.

Do not try to fry too many at a time as this will reduce the temperature of the fat and produce greasy, soggy chips.

Safety note: Always use a deep saucepan and frying basket to cook your chips. Never fill the pan more than two-thirds full of fat, and if using a gas cooker do not allow flames to rise up the sides of the pan. If your pan should catch fire DO NOT DOUSE WITH WATER, but cover with a lid or metal tray.

Potatoes Dauphinoise: slice the potatoes as thinly as possible.

POTATOES DAUPHINOISE

Hardware

potato peeler
medium-sized knife
cheese grater
large saucepan
gratin dish (ovenproof)
large shallow dish (ovenproof)

Ingredients (serves 6)

8—10 medium-sized potatoes
salt and white pepper to taste
1 small clove garlic, finely chopped
300ml/½ pint (1¼ cups) milk
300ml/½ pint (1¼ cups) double cream (heavy cream)
100g/4 ozs (4 ozs) Cheddar cheese, grated
25g/1 oz (1 oz) butter
The cheese and garlic are optional and can be adjusted to taste.

Method

1 Peel the potatoes and slice them into very thin rounds. *Do not wash them,* as the starch is needed to assist in keeping the sauce smooth.

2 Put the potatoes and the milk into a saucepan with a little salt and white pepper. Bring to the boil, lower the heat and simmer gently for 10 minutes. Add the chopped garlic and cream, and simmer for a further 2 minutes.

3 Butter an ovenproof dish, big enough to hold the potatoes. Remove the potatoes from the liquid and place them carefully into the dish. Pour the creamy liquid over, and finish by sprinkling the cheese on top.

4 Dot the top of the dish with butter. Bake at 180C/350F Gas mark 4 for 20 minutes. The top should be golden and crispy.

Stand the dish of Potatoes Dauphinoise in boiling water to prevent the cream from separating.

Parisienne Potatoes (serves 2)

1 Choose large potatoes, peel them and then, using a vegetable scoop, cut out round balls about the size of a large hazlenut. Use the bits which are left to make purée or creamed potato. You will need at least 450g/1 lb (1 lb) of potatoes to make enough balls for 2 people.

2 Put the balls into cold water, bring to the boil, cook for one minute, strain off the water and dry the potatoes over the heat in the pan, and sprinkle them with salt and white pepper.

3 To approximately 450g/1 lb (1 lb) of potato balls melt 100g/4 ozs (4 ozs) of butter until foaming. Add the balls and cook until they are golden and cooked through. This demands patience and practice, stirring the potatoes frequently with a wooden spoon and adjusting the heat to achieve the correct colour and to cook the potatoes at the same time. It will take 20-25 minutes and all your attention, but the result is worth it and you will soon become experienced enough not to have to stand over them all the time.

Sauté Potatoes (serves 2)

1 Peel 575g/1¼ lbs (1¼ lbs) of small potatoes, or if the skins are in good condition, simply wash them well. Cover them with cold salted water and bring them to the boil; cook until they are nearly done. This will take 15-20 minutes, depending on the size and type of potato. Test them with a sharp pointed knife.

2 Strain off the water and dry the potatoes in the pan with the lid on, over a gentle heat.

3 When the potatoes are cool enough to handle, cut them into slices at least 5mm/¼ inch thick. Sprinkle them with salt and freshly ground black pepper.

4 Melt 75g/3 ozs (3 ozs) of butter in a large frying pan, let it foam and then subside. Just before it starts to turn brown add the potatoes and cook over a medium-to-high heat until they are brown, and crispy bits have formed.

5 Sprinkle with chopped parsley and serve.

MAN'S MINESTRONE

Hardware

large pan or stockpot
cook's medium-sized knife
cook's large knife
cheese grater
potato peeler
wooden spoon

Ingredients (serves 8)

100g/4 ozs (4 ozs) dried butter beans
1 large carrot, roughly chopped
100g/4 ozs (4 ozs) shredded cabbage
1 medium-sized onion, roughly chopped
2—3 stalks celery (5mm/¼ inch slices)
100g/4 ozs (4 ozs) whole french beans (green beans)
100g/4 ozs (4 ozs) leeks (5mm/¼ inch slices)
100g/4 ozs (4 ozs) bacon or ham, roughly cut
100g/4 ozs (4 ozs) butter or oil
400g/14 ozs (14 ozs) can tomatoes
medium-sized peeled potato, thinly sliced
salt and black pepper to taste
3 or 4 dried bay leaves
2 × 5ml spoons/2 teaspoons (2 teaspoons) dried basil
1 × 5ml spoon/1 teaspoon (1 teaspoon) dried oregano
3 × 15ml spoons/3 tablespoons (3 tablespoons) finely chopped parsley
4 large cloves garlic
2.25 litres/4 pints (10 cups) stock (bouillon)
50g/2 ozs (2 ozs) spaghetti or any pasta

Man's Minestrone

Method

1 Soak the butter beans in cold water overnight; drain, (You could use canned ones; drain, but don't put them in the soup until the end of the cooking period.)

2 Prepare the vegetables as indicated in the list of ingredients. The canned tomatoes will benefit from a rough chop too.

3 Heat the butter or oil in a large pan, add the bacon (or ham) and cook for 5 minutes until it starts to crisp. Add the beans, herbs and vegetables, and stir so that the mixture is coated with hot fat. Season carefully, put on the lid, lower the heat, and cook gently for 10 minutes. Shake the pan frequently to prevent sticking.

4 Stir in the tomatoes and add the stock carefully. Bring the whole to the boil, then reduce the heat and simmer, uncovered, very gently for 2—3 hours. Add the pasta and cook for a further 20 minutes.

Chef's Hints

This soup is traditionally served with grated Parmesan cheese — try to get fresh Parmesan and grate it yourself.

I find that the more often this soup is cooled and re-heated the better it gets, so always make a big pot. There is nothing to stop you adding vegetables (pre-cooked) at any time in the process of manufacture, or more stock to extend it; it's a very versatile soup. Try mixing cheese (strong Cheddar or similar) into the soup before serving — it gives a very interesting characteristic.

Oxtail Soup With Dumplings

OXTAIL SOUP WITH DUMPLINGS

Hardware

very large saucepan (at least 3.40 litres/6 pints (15 cups)
cook's medium-sized knife
wooden spoon
2 mixing bowls

Ingredients (serves 4)

Soup
1 large onion
2 medium-sized carrots
50g/2 oz (2 oz) butter
2 x 15ml spoons/2 tablespoons (2 tablespoons) oil
2 x 15ml spoons/2 tablespoons (2 tablespoons) parsley, finely chopped
1 x 5ml spoon/1 teaspoon (1 teaspoon) dried thyme
1 x 5ml spoon/1 teaspoon (1 teaspoon) dried basil
1 x 5ml spoon/1 teaspoon (1 teaspoon) dried marjoram
50g/2 ozs (2 ozs) plain flour (all purpose flour)
salt and freshly ground black pepper
1 good-sized oxtail, cut into pieces
400g/14 ozs (14 ozs) can tomatoes
50g/2 ozs (2 ozs) tomato purée (paste)
300ml/½ pint (1¼ cups) red wine
1.75 litres/3 pints (7½ cups) good brown stock (bouillon)
1 large stalk celery
3 or 4 bay leaves

Suet dumplings
100g/4 ozs (4 ozs) plain flour (all purpose flour)
50g/2 ozs (2 ozs) suet
2 x 5ml spoons/2 teaspoons (2 teaspoons) baking powder
salt and white pepper to taste

Method

Soup

1. Chop the onion roughly and cut the carrots into sticks.
2. Melt the butter and oil in a large saucepan and fry the onion and carrot gently for 5 minutes.
3. Mix the herbs with the flour, add plenty of salt and freshly ground black pepper.
4. Trim any excess fat from the oxtail and roll the pieces in the herby flour. (Make sure it gets well coated).
5. Add the tail to the onions and carrots and brown the pieces evenly.
6. Add the tomatoes, tomato purée, red wine, stock, bay leaves and celery.
7. Bring to the boil, reduce the heat and simmer VERY SLOWLY until the oxtail is cooked. The longer the cooking the better the soup (about 6 hours). Stir it gently from time to time. Whilst the oxtail is cooking, make the dumplings.

Suet dumplings

1. Mix all the dry ingredients together in a bowl, add enough water to make a soft, but not wet, dough.
2. Dust your hands with flour and break the dough into small balls each about 25mm/1 inch in diameter.
3. When the oxtail is cooked, skim off any excess fat, adjust the seasoning and add the dumplings. Cook for a further 20 minutes and serve.

Chef's Hints

Small potatoes can be substituted for dumplings — or use both!

CHICKEN WITH MUSTARD

Hardware

large flameproof casserole with heavy lid
sharp medium-sized knife
wooden spoon
measuring jug
small mixing bowl
serving dish

Ingredients (serves 4)

1.5kg/3¼ lbs (3¼ lbs) chicken
2 × 15ml spoons/2 tablespoons (2 tablespoons) French mustard
1 × 15ml spoon/1 tablespoon (1 tablespoon) made-up English mustard
50g/2 ozs (2 ozs) plain flour (all purpose flour)
salt and freshly ground black pepper*
100g/4 ozs (4 ozs) butter
1 medium-sized onion, finely chopped
100g/4 ozs (4 ozs) bacon
450ml/¾ pint (2 cups) chicken stock (bouillon)
300ml/½ pint (1¼ cups) single cream (light cream)
*1 × 5ml spoon/1 teaspoon (1 teaspoon) tarragon**, basil and marjoram (mixed)*
a little extra mustard to taste (optional)

**Be very careful with salt. Remember bacon is salty, and if you use a stock cube (bouillon cube) this is also salty, so it is best not to use any extra salt until the end.*

***The herbs are optional; use a mixture as suggested, or tarragon on its own. (Dried tarragon is an excellent substitute for this delightful fresh herb).*

Method

1 Cut the chicken into 4 portions: 2 breast, 2 leg and thigh, or if you are concerned over serving all breast or leg meat, divide them further, creating 8 portions. Trim each portion, removing all loose unnecessary skin and as much bone as is practical without destroying the structure of the joint. (This skin and bone is ideal for making stock).

2 Blend the mustards together, coat each chicken piece with the mixture and then roll in seasoned flour.

3 Melt the butter in the casserole. When it is hot and just before it starts to turn brown, add the chicken pieces and fry them until they are golden brown. Remove them to a warm plate.

4 Add the bacon and onion to the casserole and fry for 5 minutes stirring with a wooden spoon and scraping up all the crispy bits into the mixture. Replace the chicken pieces into the casserole. Add the chicken stock and the herbs, cover with a close fitting lid and cook in the oven at 150C/300F Gas mark 2, for 1¼ hours.

5 Carefully remove the chicken pieces to a warm serving dish, cover loosely with foil and keep hot.

6 There should be up to 450ml/¾ pint (2 cups) of liquid left in the casserole. If it is in excess of this, boil rapidly to reduce it. Bring the whole to the boil, add the cream, adjust the seasoning and stir in a little extra mustard if you feel it needs it.

7 Pour the sauce directly over the chicken pieces and serve immediately.

Chef's Hints

Serve with baked jacket potatoes (p.22) and French beans (green beans) (p.26).

SPRING CHICKEN WITH AUBERGINE AND POTATO

Hardware

1.75-2.5 litres/3.4 pints casserole with lid
serving dish
medium-sized frying pan (skillet)
medium-sized knife
vegetable peeler
wooden spoon
tablespoon
slotted spoon
absorbent paper

Ingredients (serves 2)

575-675g/1¼-1½ lb (1¼-1½ lb) spring chicken
100g/4 ozs (4 ozs) butter
100g/4 tablespoons (¼ cup) oil
225g/8 ozs (8 ozs) potatoes
1 medium-sized aubergine (eggplant)
100g/4 ozs (4 ozs) mushrooms
1 x 15ml spoon/1 tablespoon (1 tablespoon) fresh parsley
1 x 5ml spoon/1 teaspoon (1 teaspoon) dried rosemary
1 x 2.5ml spoon/½ teaspoon (½ teaspoon) dried thyme
2 cloves garlic
6 x 15ml spoons/6 tablespoons (½ cup) chicken stock (bouillon)
salt and freshly ground black pepper

Ingredients for Chicken With Aubergine.

Method

1 Melt half the butter and half the oil in a casserole dish.

2 Cut the chicken into 8 pieces, put them into the hot oil and cook over a medium heat for 15 minutes, allowing them to become nicely brown.

3 While the chicken is cooking, peel the potato and cut it into 15mm/½ inch cubes. Melt the remaining oil and butter in a frying pan and cook the potato in it for 5 minutes, letting the cubes become well browned.

4 Slice the mushrooms and dice the aubergine (15mm/½ inch); add these to the potato and cook for a further 2 minutes.

5 Tip the vegetable mixture into the casserole with the chicken and stir the mixture together.

6 Chop the garlic and parsley finely together, then mix with the rosemary and thyme. Sprinkle this over the ingredients in the casserole and season with salt and pepper. Put the lid on the casserole and cook over a low heat for 30 minutes.

7 Remove the contents of the casserole to a warm serving dish with a slotted spoon and keep it hot in the oven. Add the stock to the pan juices left in the casserole, stirring well to mix with the juices. Remove the fat which settles on the surface with a shallow spoon and by using absorbent paper. Bring the remaining sauce to the boil, taste for seasoning and adjust if necessary. Spoon it over the chicken mixture.

Chef's Hints

Serve with a dressed green salad.

CHICKEN KIEV

Hardware

small sharp knife
rolling pin or large knife for 'batting out'
bowl for mixing butter
chip pan or other means of deep frying

Ingredients (serves 4)

breasts of two large chickens
100g/4 ozs (4 ozs) butter
2 large cloves garlic
2 x 5ml spoons/2 teaspoons (2 teaspoons) parsley
100g/4 ozs (4 ozs) plain flour (all purpose flour)
2 medium-sized eggs, whisked (beaten) together
175g/6 ozs (6 ozs) fresh white breadcrumbs

Method

1 Finely chop the parsley and garlic together and mix into the butter. Divide into four similar sized pieces and make them into cork shapes. Chill in the refrigerator.

2 Remove the skin from the chicken breast, the wings at the first joint, and any breast bone or rib cage so that you are left simply with the breast meat and the single first wing bones.

3 You will find that each breast has a small interior portion which can be detached from the main meat; do this, and very carefully, using a wet rolling pin, gently bat it out until it is as thin as a piece of paper. Wrap this round one of the corks of butter. Repeat the operation for each breast. It does not matter if it has a hole or two.

4 In a similar way, bat out the main portions of breast meat from the inside surface. It is, though, important that no holes are made in this meat.

5 Position the prepared butter so that it can be completely enveloped by the main breast meat, and form an elongated package, leaving the wing bone in its natural position.

6 Roll the package in flour, then into whisked egg and finally in breadcrumbs, patting them into position to form an even coating.

7 Heat the frying oil to 180C/350F and fry the chicken pieces until golden brown for about 20 minutes.

Above: Removing the small interior portion of meat from the chicken breast.

Above right: Wrapping the flattened interior portions around the corks of butter.

Centre right: Batting out the main portion of breast meat.

Below: A golden brown breast of chicken made succulent with garlic butter.

Beautiful!

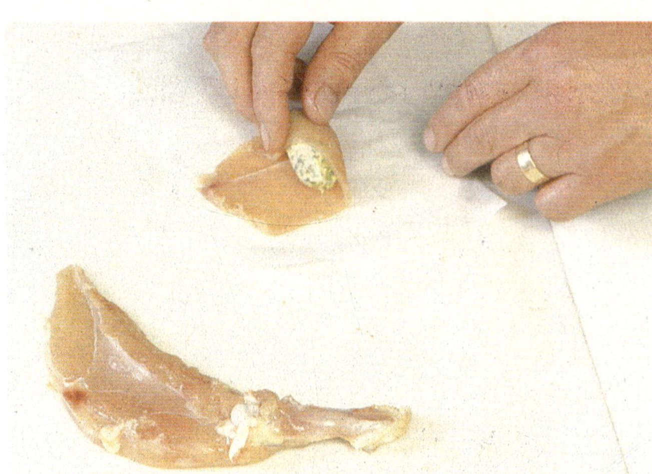

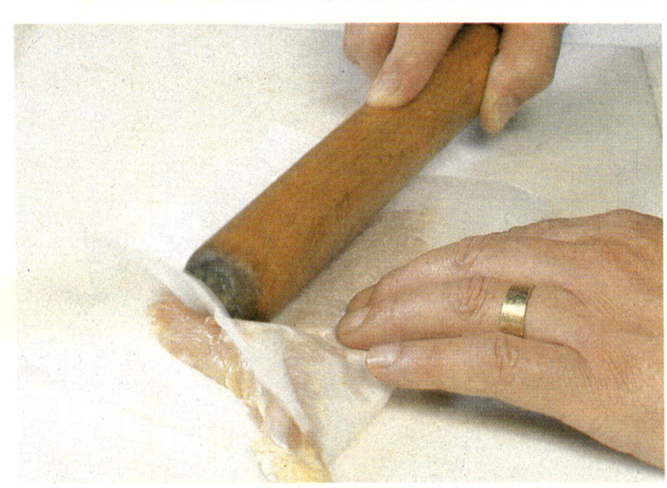

CHICKEN WITH ORANGE AND MADEIRA WINE

*Needs 2hrs. to cook the chicken, let it rest for 15mins + dish up.

Hardware

cook's medium-sized knife
large casserole dish with a close-fitting lid, enough to hold the whole chicken
saucepan
sieve
wooden spoon

Ingredients (serves 4)

2 medium-sized carrots
1 medium-sized onion
2 stalks celery
3 or 4 bay leaves
50g/2 ozs (2 ozs) butter
1.5kg/3½ lbs (3½ lbs) fresh chicken
salt and black pepper to taste
approx. 300ml/½ pint (1¼ cups) fresh orange juice
2 × 120ml/4 fl.oz. (½ cup) glasses Madeira
sugar to taste

Method

1 Prepare the carrots, onion and celery and cut them into small pieces.

2 Melt the butter in a large casserole dish, add the chopped vegetables and the bay leaves. Stir well until they are hot. Put on the lid, reduce the heat and allow to cook gently for 5 minutes.

3 Season the chicken and place it on top of the vegetables in the casserole. Pour over the orange juice and half of the Madeira wine. Put on the lid, which should be tight fitting; if not, cover the casserole first with baking foil. Cook in the oven at 190C/375F Gas mark 5 for 1 hour, or until just tender.

4 Take the chicken out of the casserole and place it in another dish. Put it back into the oven for another 15—20 minutes to brown and crisp the skin.

5 Strain the pan juices through a sieve into a saucepan. Bring them to boiling point and allow them to boil until you have only half the quantity left and juices are of a thin syrupy consistency. Add the rest of the Madeira wine, taste and adjust the seasoning with sugar, salt and pepper, or by reducing still more to concentrate the flavours.

Serve with roast potatoes + stuffing?

Inset: Cut off the meat from the tops of the rib bones, leaving the bones exposed for about 25mm/1 inch.

Above: Season the meat well and press the herbs firmly into it.

Right: Loin of Lamb served with French beans and potatoes.

LOIN OF LAMB WITH HERBS

Hardware

roasting tin
small sharp knife
medium-sized saucepan
sieve
wooden spoon
gravy boat
carving board and knife
cutlet frills

Ingredients (serves 6—8)

1.75—2.25kg/4—5 lbs (4—5 lbs) loin of lamb
salt and freshly ground pepper
75g/3 ozs (3 ozs) butter
2 x 5ml spoons/2 teaspoons (2 teaspoons) marjoram
1 x 2.5ml spoon/½ teaspoon (½ teaspoon) thyme
3 x 5ml spoons/3 teaspoons (3 teaspoons) rosemary
3 x 5ml spoons/3 teaspoons (3 teaspoons) parsley

Gravy
2 x 5ml spoons/2 teaspoons (2 teaspoons) plain flour (all purpose flour)
2 x 5ml spoons/2 teaspoons (2 teaspoons) gravy powder
450ml/¾ pint (2 cups) beef stock (bouillon)

Method

1 Ask your butcher to cut through the bone that joins the chops together.

2 Trim off the outside skin and most of the fat from the loin. Cut off all the meat from the tops of the rib bones, leaving the bone exposed for about 25mm/1 inch.

3 Season the joint well with salt and freshly ground pepper, rubbing it in well with the butter. Mix the herbs and press them into it.

4 Place the joint in a roasting dish in the oven at 190C/375F Gas mark 5, for 45 minutes. This will leave your meat pink and succulent, another 15 minutes will make it well done.

5 Remove the loin from the roasting dish and keep it hot. Mix the flour and gravy powder into the fatty pan juices, scraping in all the crispy bits and herbs. Gradually mix in 450ml/¾ pint (2 cups) of good meaty stock and bring it slowly to the boil, stirring all the time. Pour this gravy, which should be quite thin, through a sieve into a clean pan and keep it hot.

6 Place the loin on a carving board and put cutlet frills (these you can buy from most cookery shops) on the bone ends. Pour the gravy into a warm sauce boat and take to the table. Cut the loin into individual cutlets at the table and hand round the gravy separately.

SHOULDER OF LAMB WITH GARLIC

Hardware

shallow ovenproof casserole, to hold the lamb
cook's large and small knives
pan for the stock

Ingredients (serves 6)

1.5kg/3½ lbs (3½ lbs) shoulder of lamb
900g/2 lbs (2 lbs) peeled potatoes
4—6 cloves garlic
4 × 15ml spoons/4 tablespoons (4 tablespoons) parsley, finely chopped
450ml/¾ pint (2 cups) stock (bouillon) (made from a chicken stock (bouillon) cube if you wish)
50g/2 ozs (2 ozs) butter
salt and freshly ground black pepper to taste

Method

1 Trim the excess fat and any unsightly skin from meat.

2 Peel the cloves of garlic, crush one of them and rub all over the shoulder. Chop the remaining cloves very finely — like pinheads if you can.

3 Sprinkle the shoulder with salt and pepper, rub it all over with butter and press the finely chopped garlic and parsley into the butter.

4 Butter a shallow ovenproof casserole, cut the potatoes into 5mm/¼ inch slices and layer them in the casserole. Place the prepared shoulder on top of the potatoes and pour the stock over the potatoes.

5 Place the dish in an oven at 170C/325F, Gas mark 3, for 1½—2 hours, depending on whether you like your meat pink or well done.

MY MOUSSAKA

Hardware

2 large frying pans (skillets)
large casserole or earthenware dish
saucepan (for white sauce)
wooden spoons
food tongs
absorbent paper
cheese grater
cook's knife
chopping board

Ingredients (serves 6)

50g/2 ozs (2 ozs) butter
900g/2 lbs (2 lbs) cooked lamb, cut into 5mm/¼ inch cubes
2 medium-sized onions
2 cloves garlic
225g/8 ozs (8 ozs) mushrooms
400g/14 ozs (14 ozs) can tomatoes
2 × 15ml spoons/2 tablespoons (2 tablespoons) tomato purée (paste)
1-2 × 5ml spoons/1-2 teaspoons (1-2 teaspoons) dried marjoram
175g/6 ozs (6 ozs) Double Gloucester (or similar) cheese
175ml/6 fl. ozs (¾ cup) olive oil
450g/1 lb (1 lb) courgettes (zucchini)
450g/1 lb (1 lb) aubergines (eggplant)
600ml/1 pint (2½ cups) white sauce (see page 66)
salt and freshly ground black pepper

Method

1 Chop the onion and garlic finely.

2 Melt the butter in a large frying pan then add the onion and garlic and cook gently for 3-4 minutes.

3 Add the cooked, diced lamb and cook for a further 5 minutes.

4 Chop the mushrooms finely, add to the meat and onion, and stir well.

5 Roughly chop the canned tomatoes and add them with the juice to the pan.

6 Add the tomato purée, marjoram, salt and freshly ground black pepper to taste.

7 Grate the cheese and add 100g/4 ozs (4 ozs) of it to the meat mixture

8 Simmer this mixture until almost all the liquid has gone. This takes about ½ hour.

9 In the other frying pan heat the olive oil.

10 Slice the courgettes and aubergine thinly (slightly on the diagonal).

11 Fry the slices a few at a time until golden brown. Drain on the absorbent paper.

12 Line the casserole or earthenware dish with slices of courgettes and aubergines.

13 Scoop half the meat mixture into the lined dish. Cover with a layer of courgettes and aubergines. Put in the remaining meat mixture and cover with the rest of the courgettes and aubergines.

14 Pour the well-flavoured white sauce over the top so that its covers everything.

15 Sprinkle the remaining 50g/2 ozs (2 ozs) of grated cheese over the top.

16 Bake in a 180C/350F Gas mark 4, oven for about 1½ hours until the top is golden and bubbling.

SHOULDER OF LAMB WITH ANCHOVIES

Hardware

small mixing bowl
tablespoon
pestle and mortar
wooden spoon
palette knife
roasting dish
serving dish (medium-sized oval gratin dish)
kitchen paper

Ingredients (serves 6)

1.5—1.75kg/3—4 lbs (3—4 lbs) whole shoulder of lamb
1 x 5ml spoon/1 teaspoon (1 teaspoon) powdered cinnamon
1 x 15ml spoon/1 tablespoon (1 tablespoon) paprika
3 x 15ml/3 tablespoons (3 tablespoons) melted butter
2 cloves garlic
1 tin anchovy fillets (drained)
50g/2 ozs (2 ozs) soft butter
3 x 15ml spoons/3 tablespoons (3 tablespoons) brandy
1 x 2.5ml spoon/½ teaspoon (½ teaspoon) ground nutmeg
150ml/¼ pint (⅔ cup) double cream (heavy cream)

Method

1 Mix the cinnamon, paprika and melted butter together and spread over the lamb. Roast at 190C/375F Gas mark 5 for 1 hour, basting occasionally (this will give you nicely pink lamb — if you like it well done, roast for a further ½ hour).

2 Whilst the meat is cooking, chop the garlic and pound it together with the anchovies using the pestle and mortar; when this is smooth, blend in the soft butter.

3 Remove the meat from the oven and spread the anchovy paste over the top of the joint and return it to the oven for a further 30 minutes.

4 Take the lamb from the oven, place on a warm serving dish and keep it hot.

5 Skim off any excess fat from the roasting dish. When you have skimmed off as much as you can, soak up the remainder by placing a piece of kitchen paper over the surface and carefully removing it when it has absorbed as much fat as it can; repeat until it is fat free. Over a gentle heat, stir in the brandy. Add the nutmeg and cream, bring to the boil and allow to continue for 2 or 3 minutes so that it thickens slightly. Stir it all the time so that the juices are well mixed together.

6 The sauce can be poured over the joint or it can be served separately.

Chef's Hints

Serve with glazed carrots (p.29) and new potatoes (p.27) or dry roast potatoes (below).

Dry roast potatoes
Prepare as for ordinary roast potatoes, but instead of roasting them in fat, simply lightly butter a roasting dish put the potatoes in it and roast in the same oven as the meat for 1¼ hours.

My Moussaka

PORK WITH TOMATO AND GARLIC

Marmalade Roast Pork

Hardware

cook's medium-sized knife
large heatproof casserole
plate or bowl
wooden spoon
fine grater
small mixing bowl

Ingredients (serves 6)

1.25kg/2½ lbs (2½ lbs) lean pork
approx. 2 × 15ml spoons/2 tablespoons (2 tablespoons) plain flour (all purpose flour)
75g/3 ozs (3 ozs) butter
2 medium-sized onions
3 large cloves garlic
400g/14 ozs (14 ozs) can tomatoes (include the juice)
2 × 15ml spoons/2 tablespoons (2 tablespoons) tomato purée (paste)
1 × 5ml spoon/1 teaspoon (1 teaspoon) sugar
300ml/½ pint (1¼ cups) red or white dry wine
2 × 5ml spoons/2 teaspoons (2 teaspoons) oregano
salt and freshly ground black pepper to taste
1 × 15ml spoon/1 tablespoon (1 tablespoon) finely chopped parsley
1 × 15ml spoon/1 tablespoon (1 tablespoon) finely grated lemon rind

Method

1 Cut the pork into 25mm/1 inch cubes and roll them in the flour. Heat the butter in the heatproof casserole until the foam subsides, then add the pork and cook until it is evenly brown.

2 Remove the pork to a plate and set aside.

3 Finely chop the onion and garlic. Add to the casserole and cook gently for 5—6 minutes.

4 Add the tomatoes, including the juice (it is better if you break these up first — or liquidise them, if you have a liquidiser). Add the tomato purée, wine, sugar, oregano and seasonings. Bring to the boil, then reduce the heat and boil gently for 10 minutes.

5 Return the pieces of pork, mix them through the sauce, cover the casserole and place it in a pre-heated oven 180C/350F Gas mark 4, for 2½ hours or until the pork is tender.

6 Whilst the pork is cooking, mix together the grated lemon rind and parsley.

7 When the pork is cooked, taste the sauce and adjust the seasoning. The sauce should be thick. If it is not, remove the meat to a warm dish and boil the sauce rapidly to reduce and so thicken and concentrate it. Stir in the lemon and parsley mixture, replace the pork, (if you have removed it), simmer gently for 2 or 3 minutes and serve.

Chef's Hints

Serve with plain boiled rice or egg noodles and a fresh green salad. This dish can also be made with well trimmed shoulder of veal, which will probably only take about 1½ hours to cook.

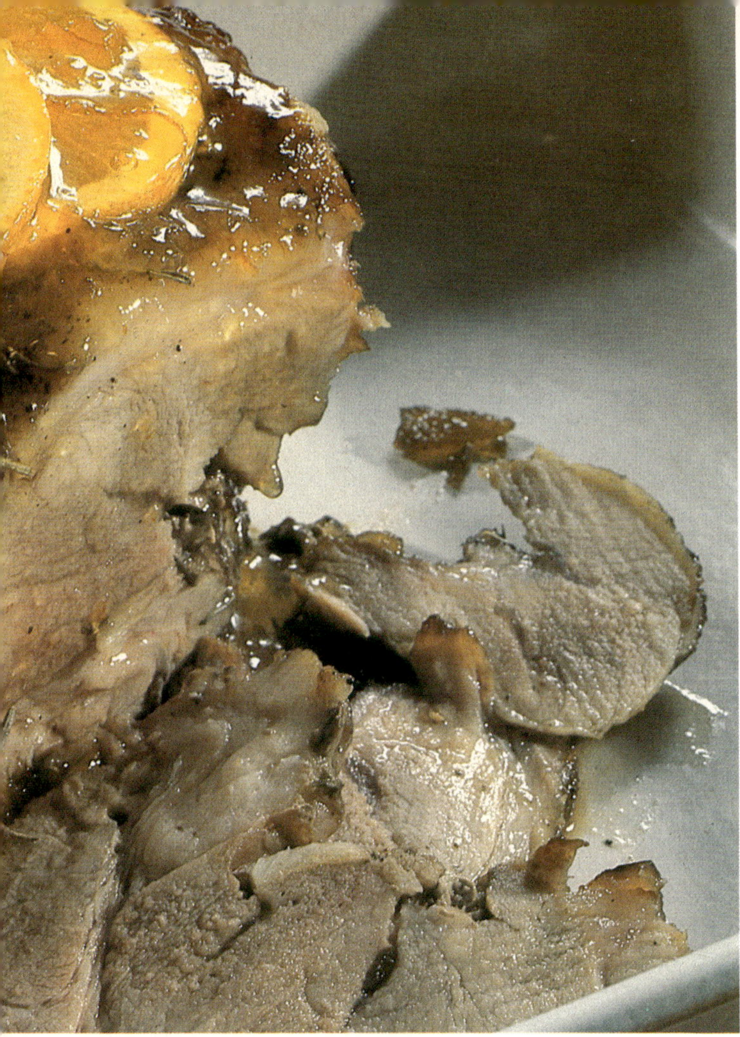

MARMALADE ROAST PORK

*Too sweet.
*Roasted @ 180°c fan, - try 170°c fan.
*Could smear with marmalade - leave out sugar + roast in tin foil.

Hardware

small sharp knife
wooden spoon
3 small mixing bowls
tablespoon
roasting pan
serving dish (oval gratin dish)

Ingredients (serves 6)

1.5—1.75kg/3—4 lbs (3—4 lbs) shoulder pork
2 cloves garlic
1 × 5ml spoon/1 teaspoon (1 teaspoon) rosemary
2 × 15ml spoons/2 tablespoons (2 tablespoons) coarse orange marmalade
2 × 5ml spoons/2 teaspoons (2 teaspoons) brown sugar
juice of 2 medium-sized juicy oranges
2 × 5ml spoons/2 teaspoons (2 teaspoons) cornflour (cornstarch)
1 × 5ml spoon/1 teaspoon (1 teaspoon) dry English mustard
1 orange for slicing

Method

1 Cut the garlic into thin slices. Make small incisions all over the piece of pork and insert the slices of garlic. Press the rosemary well into the joint, evenly distributed.

2 Place in roasting pan and roast at 190C/375F Gas mark 5, for 30 minutes per 450g/1 lb (1 lb).

3 Mix the marmalade and brown sugar together. Mix the mustard with a little of the orange juice and add to the marmalade.

4 Remove the meat from the oven and take off the rind.

5 Spread the marmalade mixture over the pork and return to the oven for a further 30 minutes. Take it out of the oven, lift the joint on top of a warmed serving dish and keep it hot.

6 Mix the cornflour with a little of the orange juice.

7 Pour any excess fat from the roasting pan or skim off with a large spoon. It is important to remove all the excess fat from the roasting pan. Use kitchen paper to absorb any that you cannot otherwise remove. Pour in the remaining orange juice and mix round the pan with a wooden spoon, stirring in all the juices and marmalade mixture (this is known as deglazing). Add the cornflour mixture and bring it to the boil, stirring well all the time. The sauce will thicken.

8 Cut the remaining orange into thin slices and arrange them over the meat. Pour the sauce over and serve.

PORK CHOPS WITH CURRY AND CIDER Excellent

It is not intended that the sauce for this recipe should be strongly curried, so, as curry powders vary in strength, please be careful adjusting the quantity to your own taste. Any cider or apple juice can be used, as a slight sweetness is required in this sauce and adjustment can be made by using more or less sugar at the end.

Hardware

vegetable peeler
frying pan (skillet)
wooden spoon
tablespoon
cook's medium-sized knife
absorbent paper
serving dish
tin foil

Ingredients (serves 2)

1 firm medium-sized eating apple
25g/1 oz (1 oz) butter
1 x 15ml spoon/1 tablespoon (1 tablespoon) vegetable oil
2 pork chops, each 25mm/1 inch thick
1 x 5ml spoon/1 teaspoon (1 teaspoon) curry powder
1 x 5ml spoon/1 teaspoon (1 teaspoon) plain flour (all purpose flour)
3 x 15ml spoons/3 tablespoons (3 tablespoons) cider
150ml/¼ pint (⅔ cup) single cream (light cream)
salt, white pepper and sugar to taste

Method

1 Peel and core a firm eating apple and cut it across into rings about 5mm/¼ inch thick; allow two rings per chop.

2 Heat the butter and oil in a frying pan, put in the apple rings and brown them lightly on each side. Put them to drain on absorbent kitchen paper until they are required.

3 Put the chops into the frying pan and cook them for 7 minutes on each side. This should just be enough to cook the chops and brown them nicely. Remove them from the pan and place in a warm serving dish. Cover with foil and put them into the oven to keep hot (the oven should be no hotter than 100C/200F (very low gas).

3 Pour off all the fat from the frying pan but try not to lose any of the meat juices. Mix the curry powder and flour into the frying pan and blend together with all the juices and bits in the pan. Add the cider, a spoonful at a time, stirring it well in, followed by the cream, creating a smooth sauce. Allow it to come to the boil and simmer gently for 3 minutes. Taste and adjust the seasoning with salt, pepper and a little sugar.

4 Put the apple rings into the sauce and cook them for 2 minutes; this is simply to heat them, not to cook them, as they are better crisp rather than soft.

5 Place the apple rings on the chops and spoon the sauce over them. The sauce should be just thick enough to coat the rings and chops thinly. If you don't think it is, reduce it a little by rapid boiling.

Pork Chops With Curry And Cider

EASY STEWED CHOPS

Hardware

shallow casserole with lid
cook's medium-sized knife
wooden spoon
medium-sized saucepan

Ingredients (serves 2)

2 × 5ml spoons/2 teaspoons (2 teaspoons) plain flour (all purpose flour)
1 × 15ml spoon/1 tablespoon (1 tablespoon) gravy powder
300ml/½ pint (1¼ cup) stock (bouillon) (made with stock (bouillon) cube)
2 large pork chops
50g/2 ozs (2 ozs) cowheel (optional)
1 medium-sized onion
1 × 2.5ml spoon/½ teaspoon (½ teaspoon) dried rosemary
pinch dried thyme
50g/2 ozs (2 ozs) lean bacon
salt and black pepper to taste

Method

1 Make your thickened gravy by mixing the flour and gravy powder with a little water and then whisking it into the slowly simmering stock in the saucepan; when it has thickened take it off the heat and put it to one side. (This should be only lightly seasoned).

2 If using the cowheel, cut it into small pieces and scatter over the bottom of a casserole dish. Place the chops on top.

3 Peel the onion and slice it into rings. Spread these over the chops. Sprinkle with the herbs and a little salt and black pepper.

4 Cut the bacon into 50mm/2 inch lengths and lay them over the onion.

5 Pour over the thickened gravy, put on the lid and place the dish in a pre-heated oven, 170C/325F Gas mark 3, for 1½ hours or until tender, removing the lid for the last 10 minutes.

Chef's Hints

Remember, before you start, cut some of the fat away. Remove any gristle or broken bones. The dish is good using stock cubes but is even better using a good home-made stock.

ESCALOPES OF PORK WITH MUSHROOMS AND CREAM

Hardware

frying pan (skillet)
wooden spoon
serving dish
cook's medium-sized knife

Ingredients (serves 4)

50g/2 ozs (2 ozs) butter
675g/1½ lbs (1½ lbs) escalopes (scallops) of pork
100g/4 ozs (4 ozs) button mushrooms
300g/½ pint (1¼ cups) double cream (heavy cream)
salt and freshly ground pepper
lemon juice to taste

Method

Your butcher will prepare the escalopes, or, alternatively buy pork fillet, cut it into 50mm/2 inch lengths, turn on end and flatten each piece.

1 Season the pork escalopes with salt and pepper.

2 Heat the butter in a frying pan until the foam subsides and gently fry the pork for about 5 minutes on each side.

3 While the pork is frying, slice the mushrooms.

4 When the pork is cooked, put it into a warm serving dish and keep hot.

5 Add the mushrooms to the pan and cook for 2 minutes.

6 Pour in the cream and stir well, scraping all the "goodness" from the bottom of the pan. Add lemon juice to taste and adjust the seasoning.

7 Bring to the boil and cook until the sauce thickens slightly — this will take several minutes.

8 Pour the sauce over the escalopes and serve.

ROAST BEEF

If well-done roast beef is your preference, this section is not for you! Roast beef in my opinion should be rare or, at the worst, medium-rare, and to this end I have never entertained with anything but the very best quality unfrozen meat. Roasting joints of beef are very expensive, but it is certainly worth paying more for top quality meat.

I prefer to roast sirloin or rib, although topside, rump and even silverside can also be roasted. However I tend to leave these cuts for braising, casseroles, mince, or perhaps for those who like overcooked roasts!

Sirloin is the cut of beef that runs from the haunch to the beginning of the ribs. It can be roasted on the bone, or boned and rolled. For traditional English sirloin, the fillet is left in, but I prefer to roast it without the fillet, because it never cooks correctly, its texture being so different from the rest of the joint. Fillet is so much better treated separately, either for steaks (particularly tournedos) or as a roast, perhaps wrapped in pastry.

Sirloin can also be used in the form of a contrefilet, which is a French cut of beef consisting of the meat which lies on the top of the sirloin, taken off the bone, trimmed of skin and gristle, and tied into shape for roasting or cut into thick slices for entrecote steaks. I consider this to be the finest cut, but it is upmarket and expensive and should be reserved for a special occasion. Boned and rolled sirloin with the fillet removed is one of the best joints for roasting. Your butcher will prepare this for you, but ask him to trim off any excess fat, skin and gristle before he rolls it.

Ribs, especially those taken from nearest the sirloin make an excellent economical joint for roasting. They can be cooked whole or boned and rolled.

Roasting Beef

Buy your beef 3 or 4 days in advance and leave to stand in a cold place until you want it, allowing it to come to room temperature before you roast it. I do not season the meat before roasting but simply spread it liberally with beef dripping, then place it on a wire grid in the roasting dish, so that the fats and juices coming from the roast during cooking do not come into contact with the meat.

The following guide gives the times and temperatures for cooking the best roasts of beef.

Boned and rolled sirloin 1.5kg/3 lbs (3 lbs) 15 minutes at 220C/425F Gas mark 7, then 14 minutes per 450g/1 lb (1 lb) at 180C/350F Gas mark 4, for rare beef, or up to 20 minutes per 450g/1 lb (1 lb) for medium-rare beef.

Rib roast with bones (2-3) ribs. 2.25-3.25 kg/5-7 lbs (5-7 lbs), 15 minutes at 220C/425F, Gas mark 7, then 15 minutes per 450g/1 lb (1 lb) at 180C/350F Gas mark 4, for rare beef, or up to 22 minutes per 450g/1 lb (1 lb) for medium beef.

Whole fillet of beef 1.5-2.25 kg/3-5 lbs (3-5 lbs) 9 minutes per 450g/1 lb (1 lb) at 220C/425F Gas mark 7, for rare beef, or up to 15 minutes per 450g/1 lb (1 lb) for medium beef.

Contrefilet 1.5 kg/3 lbs (3 lbs) in weight 15 minutes at 220C/425F Gas mark 7, for rare beef, or up to 15 minutes per 450g/1 lb (1 lb) for medium beef.

Using a sharp knife carve the meat into thin slices.

Serving roast beef

When the joint is cooked, transfer it to a carving board and leave it to stand for 15-20 minutes in a warm place. This allows the meat to set, making it easier to carve.

To make gravy, pour off as much fat from the roasting dish as you can, then mix a little flour — about 2 × 5ml spoons/2 teaspoons (2 teaspoons) — into the juices remaining in the dish, scraping in all crispy bits and pieces. Stir cold water or beef stock (bouillon) into the mixture — about 300ml/½ pint (1¼ cups). Bring it to the boil, adjust the seasoning with salt, and the thickness with more water or stock (bouillon); it should be quite thin. Add the juices that will have run from your joint of beef. Pour the gravy through a sieve into a warm sauceboat. Ensure your carving knife is sharp,and carve the meat into thin slices.

GRILLED OR FRIED STEAK

When buying a good steak, the beef should be dark red and lightly veined with fat which should be creamy white in colour. The meat and fat should be firm and moist-looking and the grain of the meat should be rather coarse. Always try to get the butcher to cut your steak to a decent thickness. (I do not think there is any point in grilling steaks less than 25mm/1 inch thick). Don't let the butcher start cutting thickly and gradually taper off to nothing — beef is expensive so make sure you get what you want!

Do not buy beef if it is pale in colour, flabby, wet and running with moisture or weak blood, with yellow fat if the meat is bright red, or tenderised beef.

Don't worry unduly if parts of a cut in the butcher's shop look a little dried, so long as the flesh looks good when carved. It is an indication that the meat has probably been 'hanging' for some time and will be all the better for it.

Dry frying is my favourite method of cooking steaks. There are special pans available for this method with ribbed bases, which, in addition to providing good heat distribution, give an attractive appearance to the finished steak. It is not, however, essential to have this type of pan and good results can be obtained with any good quality heavy frying pan (skillet).

To prepare your steak

1 It should be at room temperature, *not* straight from the fridge.

2 Trim off excess fat and any skin or gristle. Don't worry if you appear to be wasting a lot; it is better to serve a smaller steak and see every bit eaten and enjoyed, than one from which your guest has to cut away tough pieces or chew at it for minutes on end. Most people also dislike fat, so don't leave that on either, unless you know a person's taste.

3 Season the meat with freshly ground black pepper a couple of hours before you cook it, but do not salt it until the last moment. (I like to use a little paprika as well as the black pepper).

Frying steaks

1 Place your pan on the heat (do not grease it at this stage) and allow it to become very hot — water dripped on to it will bounce and sizzle.

2 Now grease the pan, but not too heavily. I find this easiest to do by soaking a wad of kitchen paper in oil and wiping it over the interior of the pan; it will quickly start to smoke so put in the steaks and seal each side rapidly. This will take two minutes each side (included in the cooking times given below).

3 Reduce the heat slightly and continue to cook in accordance with the chart below to achieve your desired degree of cooking. With a little experience you will be able to adjust your cooking and turning to achieve an attractive criss-cross pattern on your steak (if you are using a special pan).

4 Put a lump of butter, either plain or flavoured, on to the steak as you serve it, so that it is just starting to melt as it is placed before your guest.

Steak	Weight	Thickness	Cooking time each side
Fillet	175g/6 ozs (6 ozs)	30mm/1¼ inch	4 minutes rare 6 minutes medium
Rump or Sirloin	225g/8 ozs (8 ozs)	25-30mm/1-1¼ inch	3 minutes rare 5 minutes medium
T-Bone	400g/14 ozs (14 ozs)	30mm/1¼ inch	3-4 minutes rare 5-6 minutes medium

The times cannot be absolutely specific as so much depends on a person's interpretation of rare or medium and, of course, the quality and temperature of the meat. However, assuming your steaks are at room temperature before frying, the above timings should be reasonably accurate. Also, allow your steaks, after cooking, to stand in a warm place for 2—3 minutes before serving. This is particularly important in the case of rare steaks, when the heat takes a little longer than the cooking time to penetrate to the centre.

Seal the steaks for 2 minutes on each side and continue to fry until cooked to your liking.

Grilling steaks
The normal domestic grill does not get hot enough to cook steaks to perfection but it is a method of cooking that can be tried. Treat the steaks as already outlined. Make your grill as hot as you can get it and put the steaks as close to it as you can, with safety, increasing the cooking time by approximately 25% in each instance.

Various types of special butter can be served with grilled steaks, putting a slice on top of the steak and allowing it to melt over the steak as it is served.

Flavoured butter for steaks
The method of making these special, flavoured butters is simply to pound the ingredients together, then chill until firm. To make enough for 4 steaks, use 100g/4 ozs (4 ozs) butter plus one of the following: 50g/2 ozs (2 ozs) Stilton (or any similar) cheese; 2 large cloves of finely chopped garlic and 1 x 15ml spoon/1 tablespoon (1 tablespoon) finely chopped fresh parsley; 1 small tin of anchovy fillets; 2 x 5ml spoons/2 teaspoons (2 teaspoons) Dijon OR made up English mustard. To make liver pâté butter use only 75g/3 ozs (3 ozs) butter and 75g/3 ozs (3 ozs) smooth liver pâté. Best results are obtained by using unsalted butter.

FILLET STEAK IN A COVERED POT

This steak will not be rare, but the flavour will be absolutely marvellous!

Hardware

frying pan (skillet)
cook's medium-sized knife
small mixing bowl
2 individual heatproof cooking pots or casseroles
spoon
tin foil

Ingredients (serves 2)

1 x 5ml spoon/1 teaspoon (1 teaspoon) tomato purée (paste)
1 x 2.5ml spoon/½ teaspoon (½ teaspoon) dry English mustard
Good pinch ground ginger
1 x 15ml spoon/1 tablespoon (1 tablespoon) Worcestershire sauce
25g/1 oz (1 oz) butter
1 small onion
2 well-trimmed fillet steaks, 175g/6 ozs (6 ozs) each
1 x 15ml spoon/1 tablespoon (1 tablespoon) brandy

Method

1 Mix together the purée, mustard, ginger and Worcestershire sauce.

2 Heat the butter until foaming in a frying pan and cook the steaks for 1 minute only on each side — browning the outside of the meat. Place them into individual heatproof pots.

3 Chop the onion very finely, add to the juices in the frying pan and cook gently until they are soft. Add the sauce mixture and stir everything well together, allowing the mixture to get very hot. Spoon this mixture equally over the steaks in their pots, together with half the brandy to each steak.

4 Cover the pots closely with foil or a lid and place in a hot oven 220C/425F Gas mark 7, for 15 minutes.

Chef's Hints

Place the pots on the table without removing the covers — the aroma when uncovered is magnificent! Delicious with sauté potatoes or even chips (pp.32 & 33).

BOLOGNESE SAUCE

Hardware

1 large heavy frying pan (skillet) with a lid
wooden spoon
cook's knife

Ingredients (serves at least 4)

450g/1 lb (1 lb) lean, good quality minced beef (ground beef)
1 medium-sized onion
1 large clove garlic
50g/2 ozs (2 ozs) bacon
2 medium-sized carrots
450ml/¾ pint (2 cups) beef stock (bouillon) or
300ml/½ pint (1¼ cups) beef stock (bouillon), with
150ml/¼ pint (⅔ cup) red or white wine
4 × 15ml spoons/4 tablespoons (4 tablespoons) tomato purée (paste)
25g/1 oz (1 oz) butter
salt and freshly ground black pepper
1 bay leaf
1 × 5ml spoon/1 teaspoon (1 teaspoon) dried basil
1 × 5ml spoon/1 teaspoon (1 teaspoon) grated nutmeg
twist of lemon peel

Method

1 Chop the onion, garlic and carrots finely.

2 Remove the rind and dice the bacon.

3 Melt the butter in a frying pan. Add the onion, garlic, carrots and bacon and cook gently for about 5 minutes.

4 Add the minced beef and allow it to brown all over.

5 Dissolve the tomato purée in the stock and add to the mixture in the frying pan.

6 Season to taste with salt and freshly ground black pepper, and add the basil, bay leaf, nutmeg and lemon peel. Stir well, cover and simmer very gently for 30—45 minutes.

7 Uncover the pan and continue cooking for about ½ hour, until the sauce reduces and thickens slightly.

Chef's Hints

Serve on freshly cooked spaghetti.

Spaghetti can be topped with Bolognese Sauce to make a satisfying meal.

PASTA

It is very admirable to make your own pasta, but unless you have plenty of time and are reasonably skilled at pastry making, it is advisable to buy it ready-made from a delicatessen or supermarket.

The cooking of pasta is simple. Allow 75-100g/3-4 ozs (3-4 ozs) of dried pasta per person. It should be cooked in a large quantity of boiling, salted water 2.25 litres/4 pints (10 cups) to 175g/6 ozs (6 ozs) of pasta.

Most dried pasta will cook in about 15 minutes. Test it by biting a piece; it should be just a little bit firm. Strain it as soon as it is cooked, pour fresh boiling water over it and then place it in a heated serving dish ready to receive the sauce, or simply put a generous knob of butter on top and serve it with freshly grated Parmesan cheese.

When the pasta is cooked, particularly with spaghetti, instead of butter on top, put 1 × 15ml spoon/1 tablespoon (1 tablespoon) of olive oil and a finely chopped clove of garlic per person in the bottom of the serving dish. Mix the spaghetti through this and serve with grated Parmesan cheese.

Lasagne

LASAGNE

Use plain or green (verde) lasagne. The layering is only suggested, and can be arranged to suit the size of the dish.

Hardware

2.75 litres/5 pints (12 cups) saucepan for pasta
large ovenproof dish for lasagne
spoon

Ingredients (serves 6—8)

175g/6 ozs (6 ozs) lasagne (dry weight)
500g/1¼ lbs (1¼ lbs) meat filling (see opposite)
750ml/1¼ pints (3 cups) cheese sauce (see p.55).
50g/2 ozs (2 ozs) Parmesan cheese, grated
50g/2 ozs (2 ozs) butter

Method

1 Butter well a suitable container. A large, round ovenproof dish is recommended.

2 Cook the pasta as instructed on the packet. Drain and line the dish with it.

3 Spoon half the meat filling over the pasta and top this with about one-third of the cheese sauce.

4 Put in another layer of pasta and then cover it with the rest of the meat filling. Cover this with the final layer of pasta, and top with all the remaining cheese sauce.

5 Sprinkle the Parmesan cheese over the surface, dot with butter and bake until golden, for about 40 minutes in an oven at 170C/325F Gas mark 3.

MEAT FILLING

Hardware

250mm/10 inch frying pan (skillet) with lid
cook's medium-sized knife
wooden spoon

Ingredients (serves 6—8)

50g/2 ozs (2 ozs) butter
350g/12 ozs (12 ozs) minced beef (ground beef)
50g/2 ozs (2 ozs) mushrooms
2 x 15ml spoons/2 tablespoons (2 tablespoons) tomato purée
100g/4 ozs (4 ozs) bacon
1 large carrot
1 large onion
2 sticks celery
150ml/¼ pint (⅔ cup) wine (red or white)
150ml/¼ pint (⅔ cup) beef stock (bouillon)
1 clove garlic
1 x 5ml spoon/1 teaspoon (1 teaspoon) dried oregano
1 x 5ml spoon/1 teaspoon (1 teaspoon) dried basil
1 x 2.5ml spoon/½ teaspoon (½ teaspoon) ground nutmeg
150ml/¼ pint (⅔ cup) double cream (heavy cream)
salt and black pepper

Method

1 Cut the bacon into tiny pieces, put them in a large frying pan with the butter on to a low heat, and cook gently for 10 minutes.

2 Finely chop the mushrooms, carrot, onion, celery and garlic. Add to the frying pan and mix well together with the bacon. Season well with salt and pepper. Add the nutmeg and herbs and mix well, put on a lid and cook gently for another 10 minutes, stirring occasionally to prevent sticking.

3 Add the beef, tomato purée, the wine and stock. Mix well together and cook gently for 1 hour. Watch carefully and adjust the moisture with wine or stock if necessary.

4 Add the cream and mix it in well. Adjust the seasoning, adding extra herbs if you wish; allow to simmer for 15 minutes.

Chef's Hints

I find it very satisfactory to grate the carrot and celery for this recipe, instead of chopping them.

CANNELLONI

This name refers to the outer case of the pasta. The filling and sauce with which it is served vary according to a chef's whims.

Hardware

Shallow ovenproof serving dish

Ingredients (serves 6)

18 ready-made Cannelloni tubes
meat/spinach fillings (see below)
white sauce (page 66)
50g/2 ozs (2 ozs) Parmesan cheese, grated
knob of butter

Method

1 Fill the cannelloni tubes and lay them in a serving dish.

2 Pour sauce all over them and sprinkle with Parmesan cheese.

3 Dot with butter, and bake until golden brown, for 40 minutes at 170C/325F Gas mark 3.

Filling

Hardware

large saucepan with lid
medium-sized knife
wooden spoon

Ingredients

50g/2 ozs (2 ozs) butter
225g/8 ozs (8 ozs) minced (ground) beef, lamb, chicken or veal uncooked
100g/4 ozs (4 ozs) minced (ground) ham, uncooked
50g/2 ozs (2 ozs) mushrooms
1 medium-sized carrot
1 medium-sized onion
2 stalks celery
150ml/¼ pint (⅔ cup) red or white wine
150ml/¼ pint (⅔ cup) chicken or beef stock (bouillon)
225g/8 ozs (8 ozs) frozen spinach, chopped
1 x 5ml spoon/1 teaspoon (1 teaspoon) dried oregano
1 x 5ml spoon/1 teaspoon (1 teaspoon) dried basil
1 x 2.5ml spoon/½ teaspoon (½ teaspoon) ground nutmeg
salt and black pepper
100g/4 ozs (4 ozs) Cheddar cheese, grated

Method

1 Finely chop the mushrooms, carrot, onion and celery.

2 Heat the butter in a large saucepan until it foams. Add the vegetables, mix well together and season with salt and black pepper. Add the herbs and nutmeg, mix in well and cook gently with the lid on for 10 minutes, stirring occasionally to prevent sticking.

3 Add the meat, ham and stock. Mix well together, cover the pan and cook gently for 1 hour. Watch carefully, and adjust the moisture with wine or stock if necessary.

4 Add the spinach and mix it well in. Cook for a further 10 minutes, adjust the seasoning, using more herbs if you wish. Stir in the grated cheese and fill the cannelloni tubes.

MACARONI CHEESE

Left to right: Cannelloni, Lasagne, Spaghetti and Macaroni Cheese.

This is a simple and delicious pasta dish. Mix 275g/10 ozs (10 ozs) (dry weight) cooked macaroni with 750 ml/1¼ pints (3 cups) cheese sauce (recipe below). Empty this into a buttered dish, dot the surface with butter and bake until golden brown. Add variety by mixing in a little chopped and fried onion, a little cooked ham, diced, or a few slices of fresh tomato.

Cheese Sauce

Hardware

2 medium-sized saucepans
wooden spoon
cheese grater

Ingredients (serves 2—3)

50g/2 ozs (2 ozs) butter
50g/2 ozs (2 ozs) plain flour (all purpose flour)
750ml/1¼ pints (3 cups) milk
salt and pepper to taste
100g/4 ozs (4 ozs) Cheddar cheese, grated

Method

1. Melt the butter in a saucepan until it foams, add the flour and cook for 2-3 minutes over a medium heat.

2. Heat the milk in the other saucepan nearly to boiling point and gradually add to the butter and flour mixture, stirring all the time, to produce a smooth sauce. Season to taste and allow to simmer gently for 10 minutes.

3. Add the grated cheese, mix well and put to one side until needed.

HAMBURGERS

Traditionally, hamburgers should be made by using very lean top quality beef, and the recipe should contain nothing else other than seasonings. The meat mixture is shaped into round discs of about 100g/4 ozs (4 ozs) in weight, 90mm/3½ inches in diameter. They will be about 25mm/1 inch thick. They are grilled or fried in the same manner as a tender steak, 3 to 4 minutes on either side according to taste.

They are normally served sandwiched in hot buttered soft cobs, which are sometimes topped with sesame seeds. These can be bought from the more adventurous baker's shops or delicatessens. Alternatively, a muffin, barm cake or bap fulfils the need very well.

Hamburgers need not, of course, be served in a bread bun; they can make an excellent sit-down meal, served with a well-dressed crunchy salad. Perhaps give them a touch of class, and serve them with a salad of chicory (Belgian endive) and skinned segments of orange with a sweetish oil and vinegar dressing. Or with curly endive, if available, and a simple marmonde tomato salad. Marmonde tomatoes are the very large greeny-red tomatoes from the continent which are exported regularly.

Hardware

frying pan (skillet)
large knife
medium-sized knife
mixing bowl
bowls for eggs
greaseproof (wax) paper
dish or board for the hamburger

Ingredients (serves 4)

450g/1 lb (1 lb) minced (ground) rump steak
1 × 2.5ml spoon/½ teaspoon (½ teaspoon) salt
pinch freshly ground black pepper
1 egg

Method

1 Mix the ingredients together, but do not overmix as this will bind the meat too strongly together and will cause shrinkage and toughening of the cooked burger.

2 Divide into 4 pieces and shape into round balls, then flatten into 75mm/3 inch discs.

3 Grill or fry for 3—4 minutes on either side.

Chef's Hints

These freeze and defrost well. I frequently make a dozen or so, freeze them and use them for quick enjoyable snacks or supper parties. Do, however, ensure that the heat penetrates to the centre when you cook them.

Variations

Cheeseburger

Instead of putting a slice of cheese on top of the hamburger, mix 100g/4 ozs (4 ozs) of grated Cheddar cheese into the meat mixture. Cook as for the basic hamburger.

Lambburger

Replace the rump steak with 450g/1 lb (1 lb) minced (ground) leg of lamb and divide into 6, so that the discs are thinner (about 15mm/½ inch). Cook as for the basic hamburger.

Burger au poivre

Crush about 1 × 15ml spoon/1 tablespoon (1 tablespoon) of black peppercorns and pat them round the outside of the burger. Cook as normal or flambé with brandy.

To flambé, add 2 × 15ml spoons/2 tablespoons (2 tablespoons) of brandy to the pan when burger is almost cooked. The brandy will ignite when a flame is put to it. Let the brandy heat through first of all — it is the fumes from the alcohol which catch fire. A note of warning: take care!

TOMATO RELISH

Hardware

small knife
medium-sized knife
large bowl
wooden spoon
very large saucepan or stock pot
ladle

Ingredients

1.5kg/3 lbs (3 lbs) fresh tomatoes
900g/2 lbs (2 lbs) onions
100g/4 ozs (4 ozs) salt
1 × 5ml spoon/1 teaspoon (1 teaspoon) cayenne pepper
3 × 5ml/3 teaspoons (3 teaspoons) allspice, ground
1 × 5ml spoon/1 teaspoon (1 teaspoon) cloves, ground
3 × 5ml spoons/3 teaspoons (3 teaspoons) ginger, ground
4 × 5ml spoons/4 teaspoons (4 teaspoons) dry mustard
900ml/1½ pints (3¾ cups) wine vinegar
450g/1 lb (1 lb) sugar

Method

1 Peel the tomatoes and cut them in half. Peel and slice the onions. Put them in a dish, sprinkle with salt, and allow to stand overnight.

2 Drain them well, add all the spices and vinegar, place all into a large saucepan, bring to the boil, reduce the heat and simmer uncovered for 2½ hours. Add the sugar, stir well in and simmer for a further 15 minutes or so until the mixture is syrupy. Put this mixture into hot sterilized jars, leaving about 5mm/¼ inch headspace and seal.
This quantity makes about 7 × 450g/1 lb (1 lb) jam jars full.

BEAN AND BEEF STEW

Hardware

bowl for soaking beans
large saucepan
cook's medium-sized knife
large ovenproof casserole
wooden spoon

Ingredients (serves 2)

225g/8 ozs (8 ozs) dried white haricot beans
450g/1 lb (1 lb) stewing steak
1 large onion
2 large cloves garlic
50g/2 ozs (2 ozs) butter
400g/14 ozs (14 ozs) can tomatoes
150ml/¼ cup (⅔ cup) tomato juice
3 × 15ml spoons/3 tablespoons (3 tablespoons) tomato purée (paste)
salt and freshly ground pepper to taste

Method

1 Soak the beans in cold water overnight.

2 Drain the beans, put them in a saucepan with salt and cover with cold water. Bring to the boil and simmer gently for at least 30 minutes, or until tender.

3 Chop the onion and garlic quite finely.

4 Melt the butter in a large casserole, add the onion and garlic and fry gently for about 5 minutes.

5 Cut the meat into 15mm/½ inch cubes, add to the casserole and brown fairly quickly over a high heat.

6 Add the tomatoes, tomato juice (retain a little), tomato purée and mix together.

7 Add the drained beans and season generously with salt and black pepper. Cover the casserole and place in the oven at 150C/300F Gas mark 2, for about 2 hours or until the meat is cooked. About a quarter of an hour before the dish is ready, check the seasoning and add a little more tomato juice if necessary.

Chef's Hints

Serve with a fresh green salad.

STIPHADO—A RABBIT STEW FROM GREECE

Hardware

cook's medium-sized knife
large saucepan
large flameproof casserole
wooden spoon

Ingredients (serves 4)

Tomato Sauce
50g/2 ozs (2 ozs) butter
1 large onion, finely chopped
1 large clove garlic, finely chopped
approx. 575g/1¼ lbs (1¼ lbs) can tomatoes
3 × 15ml spoons/3 tablespoons (3 tablespoons) tomato purée (paste)

The Stiphado
900g-1.25kg/2—2½ lbs (2—2½ lbs) fresh rabbit
100g/4 ozs (4 ozs) butter
675g/1½ lbs (1½ lbs) small onions or shallots
½ bottle red wine
350g/12 ozs (12 ozs) home-made tomato sauce
2 or 3 bay leaves
1 × 5ml spoon/1 teaspoon (1 teaspoon) marjoram (or oregano)
1 × 5ml spoon/1 teaspoon (1 teaspoon) dried thyme
2 large cloves garlic, crushed
1 whole cinnamon stick

Method

First — make your tomato sauce

1 Heat 50g/2 ozs (2 ozs) of butter in a saucepan until it is foaming. Add the finely chopped onion and garlic and fry gently until the onion is soft (about 5 minutes).

2 Add the canned tomatoes, tomato purée and the marjoram. Bring to the boil stirring all the time, endeavouring to break up the tomatoes (you can liquidise the tomatoes before you tip them into the saucepan). Reduce the heat and allow the mixture to boil gently until the sauce is thick and homogenous. It will take about 2 hours and will need stirring occasionally.

My Lancashire Hot Pot

The Stiphado

1 Cut the rabbit into 6 joints, (discarding the head) and fry in the butter until brown. Do this in the casserole you are going to use, which must be flameproof. Remove the rabbit pieces and fry the whole onions until golden.

2 Replace the rabbit pieces, add the tomato sauce, wine, crushed cloves of garlic, cinnamon stick and herbs. Stir gently to distribute the ingredients. Bring to the boil, cover the casserole and cook in a low oven 130C/250F Gas mark ½, for at least 3 hours or until the rabbit is cooked.

3 Adjust the seasoning with salt and black pepper. The sauce should be thick, like a purée, and dark red in colour. Sometimes I allow it to go cold and reheat it the following day for about 1½ hours. The flavours impregnate the rabbit and become more concentrated. Don't worry if the rabbit falls off the bones and the onions have disintegrated — that is a Stiphado!

Chef's Hints

Serve with rough brown bread or baked jacket potatoes (p.22) and a crisp green salad.

MY LANCASHIRE HOT POT

Hardware

casserole
cook's knife
potato peeler

Ingredients (serves 4)

900g/2 lbs (2 lbs) lamp chops, middle neck
1.25kg/2½ lbs (2½ lbs) potatoes
275g/10 ozs (10 ozs) onion
150g/5 ozs (5 ozs) carrot
1 stock cube (bouillon cube)
1.15 litres/2 pints (5 cups) cold water
2 bay leaves
salt and freshly ground black pepper

Method

1 Peel the potatoes, onion and carrot and cut into 5mm/¼ inch slices.

2 Put a layer of carrots and onions into the bottom of the casserole.

3 On top of this lay half the chops.

4 Add another layer of carrot and onion and then a layer of potatoes.

5 Season well with salt and freshly ground black pepper.

6 Repeat the whole process, finishing with several layers of potatoes.

7 Season again, then add the bay leaves, stock cube and the cold water.

8 Cover and cook at 130C/250F Gas mark ½, for 3—4 hours until the meat is tender. Uncover the casserole, turn up the heat to 180C/350F Gas mark 4, for a further half an hour or until the top potatoes are crisp and nicely browned.

ANNA'S PORK CURRY

Hardware

cook's small knife
cook's medium-sized knife
large ovenproof casserole
wooden spoon
vegetable peeler

Ingredients (serves 6—8)

2 medium-sized onions
6 cloves garlic
14g/½ oz (1 small piece) fresh ginger
1 red or green pepper or ½ of each
50g/2 ozs (2 ozs) butter
4 x 15ml spoons/4 tablespoons (¼ cup) vegetable oil
1.5kg/3 lbs (3 lbs) lean pork
2 x 15ml spoons/2 tablespoons (2 tablespoons) plain flour (all purpose flour)
2 x 5ml spoons/2 teaspoons (2 teaspoons) cummin seed
4 cardomom seeds
4 whole cloves
1 x 15ml spoon/1 tablespoon (1 tablespoon) coriander
2 x 5ml spoons/2 teaspoons (2 teaspoons) paprika
2 x 5ml spoons/2 teaspoons (2 teaspoons) turmeric
1 x 5ml spoon/1 teaspoon (1 teaspoon) fenugreek
2 x 5ml spoons/2 teaspoons (2 teaspoons) ground cinnamon
600ml/1 pint (2½ cups) water or stock (bouillon)
400g/14 oz (14 oz) can tomatoes
2 medium-sized apples
100g/4 ozs (4 ozs) sultanas (seedless white raisins)
1 x 15ml spoon/1 tablespoon (1 tablespoon) curry powder
salt and pepper to taste

Method

1 Peel the onions, garlic and ginger.

2 Finely chop the onion and garlic, cut the ginger into matchlike strips.

3 Remove the seeds from the peppers and slice them thinly.

4 Heat the butter and oil in a large casserole. Add the cummin, cardomom seeds, onion, garlic and ginger and fry gently for 5 minutes, stirring occasionally.

5 Cut the pork into 25mm/1 inch cubes and sprinkle with the flour. Add them to the casserole and allow the meat to brown slightly.

6 Add the sliced peppers and the remaining spices and mix them together, then add the water or stock and bring to the boil stirring gently. Reduce the heat and allow to simmer.

7 Chop the canned tomatoes and pour them, including the juice, into the casserole.

8 Peel and core the apples, chop roughly and, together with the sultanas, add to the mixture.

9 Place the lid on the casserole and put it into a pre-heated oven. Cook at 140C/275F Gas mark 1, for approximately 2 hours or until the meat it tender.

10 Taste the sauce and adjust the seasoning if necessary.

Chef's Hints

Serve with plain boiled rice and traditional curry accompaniments, such as lime pickle, chutneys, banana, finely chopped onion with paprika, popadums, chapatis etc.

The heat of this curry is determined by the curry powder, so it is up to you how much curry powder you use. This curry freezes and re-heats very successfully.

Fried Curry Pasties

FRIED CURRY PASTIES

These are scrumptious and once you start to eat them you cannot stop — so always make plenty.

Hardware

cook's medium-sized knife
large frying pan (skillet) with lid
wooden spoon
rolling pin
small knife
pastry brush

Ingredients (makes 25—30)

1 large onion
2 large cloves garlic
50g/2 ozs (2 ozs) butter
2 cardomom seeds
2 x 5ml spoons/2 teaspoons (2 teaspoons) turmeric
2 x 5ml spoons/2 teaspoons (2 teaspoons) cummin seed
4 x 5ml spoons/4 teaspoons (4 teaspoons) curry powder
2 x 5ml spoons/2 teaspoons (2 teaspoons) ground coriander
2 x 5ml spoons/2 teaspoons (2 teaspoons) paprika
1 x 2.5ml spoon/½ teaspoon (½ teaspoon) ground cloves
2 x 5ml spoons/2 teaspoons (2 teaspoons) ginger
2 x 5ml spoons/2 teaspoons (2 teaspoons) cinnamon
450g/1 lb (1 lb) finely minced (ground) beef
tomatoe purée (paste)
juice of 1 lemon
salt to taste
450g/1 lb (1 lb) bought puff pastry
oil for frying

Method

1 Finely chop the onion and garlic and fry in the butter with the cardomom and cummin seeds until golden brown.

2 Mix in all the remaining spices with the tomato purée and cook gently for 5 minutes.

3 Add the minced meat, mix thoroughly together and cook for 5 minutes stirring all the time. Put on the lid and cook on a low heat for 25 minutes.

4 Remove the lid and continue to cook until all the liquid has evaporated — it will be necessary to stir frequently to prevent it from sticking.

5 Add the lemon juice, season to taste and allow the mixture to cool. This mixture is known as dry or keema curry.

To make the Pasties

1 Roll out the puff pastry very thinly and cut out 100mm/4 inch circles. The trimmings can be rolled out again and more circles cut until all the pastry is used. You should have 25 to 30 circles.

2 Put a heaped 5 ml spoon/teaspoon (teaspoon) of filling into the centre of each pastry disc and moisten the edges with water. Use very little water, but ensure the whole of the edge of the pastry is moist. Fold the pastry over the filling to form a halfmoon shape and seal the edges firmly.

3 Deep fry for 5 or 6 minutes.

PIZZA

DOUGH

Hardware

sieve
mixing bowl
measuring jug
baking tin (pan)
tea towel
sheet of polythene
fork
cling film

Ingredients (makes 6 × 180mm/7 inch pizzas)

450g/1 lb (1 lb) plain flour (all purpose flour)
14g/½ oz fresh yeast (½ oz cake compressed yeast)
1 egg
4 × 15ml spoons/4 tablespoons (¼ cup) olive oil
4 × 5ml spoons/4 teaspoons (4 teaspoons) salt
200ml/⅓ pint (⅞ cup) warm water

To make the pizza bases: On a floured surface divide the dough and shape the pieces into smooth balls

Method

1 Sieve the flour and salt together into a bowl.

2 Measure the warm water and mix the yeast into it.

3 Add the oil and egg to the water and beat lightly with a fork.

4 Gradually add the liquid to the flour and mix to a smooth dough.

5 Divide the dough into six pieces and shape them into smooth balls.

6 Stand the pieces of dough on a lightly greased baking tin, cover with a damp tea towel and stand in a warm place to rise for 1 hour. A warm airing cupboard is usually a suitable place.

7 Roll the pieces out to about 5mm/¼ inch thick, cover with a sheet of polythene and allow to stand for a further 15 minutes.

8 Spread with tomato base and topping (see opposite) and allow to stand for another 15 minutes.

9 Bake at 220C/425F, Gas mark 7, for 15 minutes.

10 Serve immediately with a crisp green salad.

Chef's Hints

Pizzas freeze and re-heat very well. To do this carry on until you have covered the dough with your chosen topping, *but* bake at only 200C/400F, Gas mark 6 for about 15 minutes; the base edges should just be showing colour. Let them cool, wrap them in cling film, place in a polythene bag and freeze them. To re-heat, remove from the polythene bag, take off the cling film, and re-heat at 230C/450F Gas mark 8, for about 10 minutes.

TOPPINGS

These are legion and you can enjoy a very wide choice, as specialist pizza restaurants demonstrate. The following are suggestions for ingredients which can be used. 50g/2 ozs (2 ozs) of either of the following or a combination of your choice: onions, mushrooms, red and green peppers (these should be softened slightly in hot oil or butter for about 5—7 minutes before using as a topping).

You can also choose from chopped, boiled ham, olives, anchovies, salami, garlic sausage, spicy sausage, mussels, cockles, prawns, shrimps, cooked, minced (ground) lamb or beef.

Right: Pizzas with anchovy and olive topping.

TOMATO BASE

Hardware

large saucepan
wooden spoon
palette knife

Ingredients

25g/1 oz (1 oz) butter
2 large cloves garlic
1.5kg/3½ lbs (3½ lbs) canned Italian plum tomatoes
2 × 5ml spoons/2 teaspoons (2 teaspoons) sugar
1 × 5ml spoon/1 teaspoon (1 teaspoon) salt
pinch of black pepper
1 × 5ml spoon/1 teaspoon (1 teaspoon) dried basil
1 × 5ml spoon/1 teaspoon (1 teaspoon) dried oregano
1 × 2.5ml spoon/½ teaspoon (½ teaspoon) dried thyme
175g/6 ozs (6 ozs) mozzarella or cheese of your choice (25g/1 oz (1 oz) per base)
350g/12 ozs (12 ozs) topping of your choice (50g/2 ozs (2 ozs) per base)

Method

1 Melt the butter in a saucepan, finely chop the garlic, add to the butter and cook for 1 minute.

2 Chop up the tomatoes in their juice and add them to the butter. Then mix in the herbs, sugar and seasoning.

3 Cook over a high heat, stirring frequently, until all the liquid has evaporated: a thick purée is left. Adjust the seasoning and allow to cool.

4 Spread the purée generously over the 6 pizza bases.

5 Distribute the topping (see opposite) over the tomato, and grate cheese to cover it; you can also sprinkle on a few extra herbs if you wish.

6 Cook in a hot oven 220C/425F Gas mark 7, until the base edges are brown and the topping mixture is bubbling, for about 15 minutes.

STEAK AND KIDNEY PIE

Hardware

oval pie dish (600ml/1 pint (2½ cups)
mixing bowl
small bowl
pallette knife
rolling pin
medium-sized knife
polythene or tin foil
pastry brush

Ingredients (serves 3)

175g/6 ozs (6 ozs) plain flour (all purpose flour)
75g/3 ozs (3 ozs) lard (shortening)
1 × 2.5ml spoon/½ teaspoon (½ teaspoon) salt
2 × 5ml spoons/2 teaspoons (2 teaspoons) baking powder
4 × 15ml spoons/4 tablespoons (¼ cup) cold water
the quantity of steak and kidney filling (p. 65)
1 small egg for glazing

Method

1 Sieve the flour, salt and baking powder into the mixing bowl.

2 Rub in the lard until the mixture resembles fine breadcrumbs.

3 Gradually mix in the water using a palette knife until it forms a block of pastry. Shape it into a flat sphere, wrap in polythene or tin foil and keep in the refrigerator until required.

4 Tip the cold filling into the pie dish.

5 Roll out the pastry to fit the dish, it should be about 5mm/¼ inch thick. Make two or three cuts in it.

6 Beat the egg and brush the edges of the pie dish with it. Position the pastry lid, seal the edges, and trim off any surplus. This can be used to make leaves for decoration.

7 Brush the pastry with the remaining egg and bake at 220C/425F Gas mark 7, for 40-45 minutes, until golden brown.

STEAK AND KIDNEY PUDDING

Hardware

sieve
600ml/1 pint (2½ cups) basin
mixing bowl
rolling pin
palette knife
greaseproof (wax) paper or linen square
string
steamer or large saucepan

Ingredients (serves 2)

100g/4 ozs (4 ozs) plain flour (all purpose flour)
50g/2 ozs (2 ozs) shredded (chopped) beef suet
2 × 5ml spoons/2 teaspoons (2 teaspoons) baking powder
1 × 2.5ml spoon/½ teaspoon (½ teaspoon) salt
3 × 15ml spoons/3 tablespoons(3 tablespoons) cold water
the steak and kidney filling (see page 65)

Method

1 Sieve the flour and baking powder into a bowl.

Succulent Steak and Kidney Pie.

2 Mix the salt and beef suet through the flour, then gradually stir in the cold water to form a soft pastry.

3 Divide the pastry into two pieces, one being 3 times the size of the other. Roll out the larger piece and line the pudding basin, leaving a rim to which you can attach the pastry lid.

4 Fill the lined basin with the cold steak and kidney filling.

5 Roll out the remaining pastry to form a lid, dampen the edges, position the lid and seal the edges firmly together.

6 Cover the basin with greaseproof paper or with a piece of clean linen (pleated in the middle to allow the crust to rise). Tie the cover well down to prevent moisture making the pastry wet.

7 Cook the pudding in a steamer for 1½ hours. Alternatively, stand the pudding in a large saucepan and pour in boiling water to come half-way up the side of the basin. Cover with a lid and cook for 1½ hours.

STEAK AND KIDNEY FILLING

Hardware

1 heavy casserole
medium-sized knife
jug or bowl
wooden spoon

Ingredients (serves 2—4)

450g/1 lb (1 lb) stewing steak
100g/4 ozs (4 ozs) kidneys
1 small onion
1 beef stock (bouillon) cube
750ml/1¼ pints (3 cups) water
salt and freshly ground black pepper

Optional thickening
2 x 5ml spoons/2 teaspoons (2 teaspoons) plain flour (all purpose flour)
2 x 5ml spoons/2 teaspoons (2 teaspoons) gravy powder

Blend the above together with approximately ½ tea cup of cold water. If it is preferred thicker, simply increase the flour quantity a little.

Method

1 Cut the steak and kidneys into 15mm/½ inch cubes and put into a heavy casserole.

2 Chop the onion and add to the casserole with the stock cube, water and just a little salt and pepper.

3 Cover the casserole and cook very slowly in the oven for 4-5 hours at 130C/250F Gas mark ½, until the meat is tender.

4 When the meat is cooked, thicken the gravy if desired by adding the blended flour and gravy powder to the casserole. Stir well, bring to the boil, and simmer for a further few minutes. Allow to cool.

Chef's Hints

Add two or three medium-sized carrots and 175g/6 ozs (6 ozs) of chopped mushrooms (the larger ones give the best flavour) to give variety with the onion.

This filling can be served as it is with chips.

WHITE SAUCE

Hardware

2 medium-sized saucepans
wooden spoon

Ingredients

600ml/1 pint (2½ cups) milk
1 medium-sized onion
3 cloves
50g/2 ozs (2 ozs) butter
50g/2 ozs (2 ozs) plain flour (all purpose flour)
salt and white pepper

Method

1 Peel the onion, stud it with cloves and put it in a saucepan.

2 Pour the milk over the onion, bring to the boil and simmer gently for about 20 minutes. Remove the studded onion and discard.

3 Melt the butter in the other saucepan, add the flour and stir well; cook for 1 minute.

4 Add the warm milk a little at a time, mixing well and allowing to boil between each addition of milk.

5 Season to taste with salt and white pepper.

Chef's Hints

If you wish to make this sauce in advance, when it is finished cover the surface with very thin slices of butter which will melt and prevent a skin forming, and will easily mix in when the sauce is reheated.

CHICKEN AND HAM PIE

Hardware

medium-sized mixing bowl
wooden spoon
medium-sized knife
250mm/10 inch pie plate
rolling pin
brush for egg glaze
1 small mixing bowl
pastry brush

Ingredients (serves 4-6)

175-225g/6-8 ozs (6-8 ozs) chicken meat, cooked
175-225g/6-8 ozs (6-8 ozs) ham, cooked
600ml/1 pint (2½ cups) white sauce (see opposite)
pinch ground nutmeg
1 × 15ml spoon/1 tablespoon (1 tablespoon) fresh parsley, finely chopped
575g/1¼ lbs (1¼ lbs) shortcrust pastry
small egg for glazing

Method

1 Cut the chicken and ham into 5mm/¼ inch cubes.

2 Fold the meat into the white sauce (see left) with the nutmeg and parsley. Set aside and allow to cool.

3 Take half the pastry, and roll it out to fit the plate and line it carefully; trim off the excess and spread the meat and sauce filling over the base.

4 Put the trimmings with the remaining pastry and roll that out to form the lid. Make 3 or 4 cuts in the pastry lid 100mm/4 inches long.

5 Moisten the edges of the base with water, position the lid to cover the filling and seal the edges together, making a fancy edge by squeezing it between finger and thumb.

6 Brush the surface with beaten egg and bake at 200C/400F Gas mark 6, for 45 to 50 minutes.

LAMB PIE WITH SPINACH

Hardware

Frying pan (skillet) with lid
wooden spoon
cook's knife
plain flan ring, 180mm/7 inches diameter
baking tin (pan)
rolling pin
saucepan
pastry brush
strainer
serving plate
baking sheet

Ingredients (serves 4—6)

50g/2 ozs (2 ozs) butter
1 medium-sized onion
450g/1 lb (1 lb) lamb (lean shoulder meat)
14g/½ oz (½ oz) plain flour (all purpose flour)
salt and freshly ground black pepper
3 x 15ml spoons/3 tablespoons (3 tablespoons) spinach, chopped
400g/14 ozs (14 ozs) can tomatoes
2 x 5ml spoons/2 teaspoons (2 teaspoons) ground coriander
150ml/¼ pint (⅔ cup) gravy or stock (bouillon)
1 recipe Fruit Pie Pastry (p. 75)
1 egg, whisked (beaten) for glazing

Method

Filling

1 Melt the butter in the frying pan; chop the onion and cook gently for 3-4 minutes.

2 Cut the lamb into 15mm/½ inch cubes, season well with salt and freshly ground black pepper, and coat with flour.

3 Turn up the heat and add the lamb to the frying pan, together with any surplus flour. Brown the meat all over, stirring continually so that the flour does not stick. Add the spinach and mix.

4 Strain the tomatoes from their juice, chop roughly and add to the pan. Add the coriander, the gravy or stock and the juice from the tomatoes, mixing well, until it becomes a smooth, thick sauce. Cover and simmer gently for about 45 minutes.

5 Strain the sauce into a pan. Allow the sauce and the meat to cool.

Lamb Pie

Pie

1 Divide the pastry into two pieces, one nearly twice as large as the other.

2 Lightly grease a baking sheet and a flan ring, and stand the ring on the sheet.

3 Roll out the larger pastry piece to about 300mm/12 inches in diameter, pick it up by rolling it around the rolling pin, and lay it gently over the flan ring.

4 Shape the pastry to the inside of the ring, pressing it down evenly and gently to fit the contours of the flan.

5 Remove surplus pastry from the top of the ring, but leave some overlapping the rim.

6 Add the trimmings to the remaining pastry, roll it out to a size sufficient to cover the top of the flan ring, and make small cuts in its surface.

7 Empty the prepared and cooled filling into the lined ring, moisten it with a little of the sauce and spread it level.

8 Moisten the rim of the lower pastry circle, place the second circle on to it, and squeeze the two rims together, sealing in the filling completely.

9 Brush the top with whisked egg and bake at 200C/400F Gas mark 6, for about 1 hour and 10 minutes.

10 Remove the pie from the ring and serve with the sauce, which should be re-heated.

KEDGEREE

Hardware

frying pan (skillet)
medium-sized saucepan
chopping board
sieve
large knife
wooden spoon
plate
serving dish

Ingredients (serves 2)

approx. 150ml/¼ pint (⅔ cup) milk
350g/12 ozs (12 ozs) smoked haddock or cod
50g/2 ozs (2 ozs) long-grain rice
50g/2 ozs (2 ozs) butter
2 eggs, hard-boiled
1 × 5ml spoon/1 teaspoon (1 teaspoon) curry powder
1 × 15ml spoon/1 tablespoon (1 tablespoon) parsley, finely chopped
1 lemon
salt and freshly ground pepper

Method

1 Put the fish into the frying pan and pour in enough milk to cover. Bring slowly to the boil and simmer gently for about five minutes. Drain and flake the fish, removing any bones and bits of skin. The milk is unfortunately not used in this dish, but the family pet would probably appreciate it. Put the flaked fish on to a plate and reserve.

2 Place the rice into a sieve and wash well with cold water. Pour into about 1.15 litres/2 pints (5 cups) of boiling, salted water and cook for 7 minutes. Drain in the sieve and then pour a kettle of boiling water over the rice — this removes any excess starch and leaves the rice dry and fluffy. Reserve for later use.

3 Melt the butter in the frying pan, add the curry powder and mix well. When the butter starts foaming, add the flaked fish and rice and heat gently.

4 Meanwhile, chop the hard-boiled eggs roughly and add to the frying pan.

5 Stir in the finely chopped parsley, season to taste with salt and pepper and mix well. Empty into a warmed serving dish and decorate with the lemon cut into wedges.

SHALLOW FRYING FISH

This method of cooking is known as à la meunière. It can of course be used for any fish, whole, filleted or in steaks, and is particularly suitable for flat fish such as sole or plaice. This is an admirable way of cooking trout or a thick steak of hake or halibut.

The fat to use is butter, but unfortunately it will burn unless clarified first, resulting in your fish being covered with black flecks of burnt butter. However, it is not difficult to clarify butter. Melt the butter in a small saucepan: you'll need about 100g/4 ozs (4 ozs) for a medium-sized plaice. Let it get quite hot then put it to one side for a minute or so; you will then see that the salt and milk solids have separated and fallen to the bottom of the pan, forming a whitish sediment. You can, with care, pour the clear yellow butter fat off, or you can strain it through a clean white muslin (cheesecloth). It is this butter fat which you use to cook the fish.

Having prepared the butter, put it into a shallow frying pan to heat. Meanwhile, sieve a little salt and white pepper into plain white flour (all purpose flour) and dip the fish into this. Coat the fish thinly and evenly all over, and shake off any surplus flour. Put the fish into the hot butter and fry gently until golden brown. The timing depends on how thick the fish is, but when it is done it will flake easily when pierced gently with a fork.

Now heat a further 75g/3 ozs (3 ozs) of unclarified butter in another pan. Shake the pan to enable the butter solids to brown evenly, then pour it, foaming and golden, over your fish. Garnish with quarters of lemon and serve immediately.

Trout with Almonds
Cook trout as above. I like to add 50g/2 ozs (2 ozs) of flaked almonds to the pouring butter. Let them become golden brown and then cover the trout with this delicious nutty, buttery mixture.

Hake or Halibut with Parsley Butter
For steaks of hake or halibut the pouring butter can be omitted and, instead, you can make some parsley butter by finely chopping a few sprigs of parsley to make enough to fill 1 × 15ml spoon/1 tablespoon (1 tablespoon) and mixing this into 50g/2 ozs (2 ozs) of butter. Put this on top of the hot fish, letting it melt into it as it is served.

Plaice fried in butter, garnished with lemon and parsley.

FISH ON SKEWERS

I consider this to be one of the most enjoyable ways to eat fish, particularly if you can cook the fish over charcoal. The only restrictions on the type of fish used are that it must be firm and fleshy, and reasonably easy to remove from the bones. Many fish fall into this category; amongst the most suitable and readily available are: hake, halibut, turbot, monkfish, salmon, shark and good fresh cod or haddock

Hardware

8 skewers, 150mm/6 inches long
sharp medium-sized cook's knife
bowl for marinade

Ingredients (serves 4)

575g/1¼ lbs (1¼ lbs) fish
1 medium-sized red or green pepper
2 medium-sized onions
12 small firm tomatoes

Marinade

150ml/¼ pint (⅔ cup) olive oil
juice of one lemon or lime
2 × 5ml spoons/2 teaspoons (2 teaspoons) dried oregano
1 × 5ml spoon/1 teaspoon (1 teaspoon) dried thyme
1 × 15ml spoon/1 tablespoon (1 tablespoon) parsley, dried or chopped
2 large cloves garlic
1 × 2.5ml spoon/½ teaspoon (½ teaspoon) salt
freshly ground black pepper

Method

1. Remove the skin and bones from the fish and cut it into 25mm/1 inch cubes.

2. Make the marinade simply by mixing all the marinade ingredients together. Soak the fish pieces in the marinade for at least 1 hour.

3. Quarter the onions, peppers and tomatoes into pieces suitable for skewering between the pieces of fish.

4. Starting with onion, skewer the fish and vegetables, alternating them as you wish, but start and finish with onion as this holds the other items firmly in position. Fill the skewers well but not too tightly.

5. Spoon a little marinade over the skewers and grill under a pre-heated (hot) grill for 10—12 minutes. Turn them occasionally and baste with marinade.

Chef's Hints

These are delicious grilled over charcoal but be careful when basting.

Serve with plain boiled rice and lemon or garlic butter, or tomato relish (p. 57).

Lemon butter Soften but do not melt 100g/4 ozs (4 ozs) unsalted butter, and gradually mix in the juice of a large juicy lemon.

Garlic butter Chop two large cloves of garlic and crush them to a paste. Mix with 100g/4 ozs (4 ozs) of softened butter.

GRILLED MACKEREL

Hardware

food tongs
grill pan (broiler pan)

Ingredients (serves 3)

2 medium-sized mackerel
25g/1 oz (1 oz) butter

Method

1 Ask your fishmonger to clean the mackerel and remove the heads.

2 Wash and dry the fish, place them on the wire rack in the grill pan, and dot with half the butter.

3 Grill (broil) for 5—6 minutes, then turn the fish, dot with the remaining butter and cook for a further 5—6 minutes.

4 Serve with a separate mustard sauce.

Mackerel should be bought very fresh, the skins should be shiny and the eyes bright.

MUSTARD SAUCE

Hardware

saucepan
wooden spoon

Ingredients (serves 3)

20g/¾ oz (¾ oz) butter
20g/¾ oz (¾ oz) plain flour (all purpose flour)
300ml/½ pint (1¼ cups) milk
ready-mixed mustard
salt and white pepper to taste

Method

1 Melt the butter in the saucepan. When it is foaming, add the flour and mix well. Cook for about 1 minute without browning.

2 Add the milk a little at a time, mixing well and allowing the sauce to come gently to the boil between each addition of milk.

3 Season to taste with salt and white pepper and simmer gently for 2—3 minutes.

4 Add mustard to your own taste. I find that 1—2 x 5ml spoons/1—2 teaspoons (1—2 teaspoons) is usually about the right amount.

Fish pie garnished with prawns.

FISH PIE WITH LIGHT CHEESE SAUCE

Hardware

medium-sized saucepan
wooden spoon
cheese grater
shallow ovenproof serving dish
cook's medium-sized knife
piping bag (pastry bag) or palette knife

Ingredients (serves 2)

Light cheese sauce
25g/1 oz (1 oz) butter
25g/1 oz (1 oz) plain flour (all purpose flour)
450ml/¾ pint (2 cups) milk
salt and white pepper to taste
50g/2 ozs (2 ozs) Cheddar cheese, grated

Fish Pie
450g/1 lb (1 lb) fish
450g/1 lb (1 lb) mashed potato
25g/1 oz (1 oz) Cheddar cheese, grated

Method

1 Prepare your fish by removing the skin and bone and cutting it into 15mm/½ inch cubes. Put it to one side.

2 Make the sauce: melt the butter in a saucepan, stir in the flour and cook gently for two minutes, stirring all the time.

3 Add the milk a little at a time, mixing it into the roux until all the liquid is incorporated. Bring to the boil stirring constantly until the sauce is smooth and thick. Remove from the heat, and stir in the grated cheese. Adjust the seasoning with salt and pepper.

4 Add the fish to the sauce and allow to simmer gently for 2—3 minutes, stirring very carefully all the time. Pour this mixture into a shallow buttered ovenproof dish and allow it to cool.

5 Spread the mashed potato over the top of the fish filling. This is best done with a piping bag, but with care can be done with a palette knife. It can be put on in spoonfuls, making sure that the fish/sauce mixture is completely covered.

6 Spread the grated cheese over the potato topping and bake at 190C/375F Gas mark 5, for 20 minutes or until the top is golden brown.

Chef's Hints

Suitable fish are cod, haddock, hake, but for a superior pie use halibut and salmon.

A few prawns (shrimp) added to the mixture give a little extra interest; for a superb pie try a mixture of salmon and lobster meat.

MERINGUES

Hardware

large spotlessly clean bowl
balloon whisk or an electric whisk
baking tray
large spoon
palette knife
piping bag (pastry bag) (optional)
(Everything, except the baking tray, must be free from grease!)

Ingredients (serves 4)

egg whites from 3 medium-sized eggs
200g/7 ozs (7 ozs) caster sugar (granulated sugar)
300ml/½ pint (1¼ cups) double cream (heavy cream), whipped

Method

1 Prepare the baking tray by lightly greasing it with lard or cooking fat and then coating it thinly with flour.

2 Whisk the egg whites on their own in the bowl until they form soft peaks.

3 Gradually add the caster sugar, carefully whisking it in until you have added about ⅔ of it. Then whisk until the mixture is very stiff. Carefully fold in the remaining sugar.

4 Spoon out the mixture on to the prepared baking tray into 8 equal amounts; get them as even as you can, but don't worry unduly.

5 Bake at 130C/250F, Gas mark ½, until tinged with brown and firm to the touch, about 1½ hours. Do not remove from the oven but switch off the heat and allow to get cold, or nearly cold.

6 Using a palette knife, remove the meringues carefully, making a hole in the flat base as you do so.

7 Using a piping bag or spoon, fill the meringue shells with whipped cream, piling it high, then push pairs of filled shells together.

Chef's Hints

Serve these delicious meringues on individual plates or dishes with a bowl of sweetened raspberries or strawberries, from which people can help themselves.

BOOZY BANANAS

Hardware

large frying pan (skillet)
knife
wooden spoon
box of matches

Ingredients (serves 2—4)

4 firm bananas, sliced in half, lengthwise
50g/2 ozs (2 ozs) butter
2 × 15ml spoons/2 tablespoons (2 tablespoons) demerara sugar (light brown sugar)
150ml/¼ pint (⅔ cup) fresh orange juice
1 × 15ml spoon/1 tablespoon (1 tablespoon) each, Cointreau and Cognac.

Method

1 Heat the butter in the frying pan until it foams. Add the bananas and cook gently, allowing them to take a little colour, for 5 minutes.

2 Add the orange juice and the demerara sugar, mix carefully and boil rapidly so that a thickish syrupy sauce is formed.

3 Pour in the Cointreau and Cognac and allow it to burn, if you are cooking on gas, or set light to it with a match. (Be careful if you have not done this before). Serve immediately.

Above: Preparing and serving Bread and Butter Pudding.

Below: Boozy Bananas.

BREAD AND BUTTER PUDDING

Hardware

1 medium-sized ovenproof dish
mixing bowl
saucepan
wooden spoon
roasting pan
whisk

Ingredients (serves 2)

2 large eggs
40g/1½ ozs (1½ ozs) caster sugar (granulated sugar)
3 large, thin slices of bread and butter
50g/2 ozs (2 ozs) sultanas (seedless white raisins)
600ml/1 pint (2½ cups) milk
1 × 5ml spoon/1 teaspoon (1 teaspoon) sugar

Method

1 Butter the dish.

2 Cut the crusts from the bread and butter and cut the slices into quarters.

3 Layer the bread and butter in the dish, sprinkling the layers with sultanas.

4 Beat together the eggs, caster sugar and about 3 × 15ml spoons/3 tablespoons (3 tablespoons) of the milk.

5 Heat the rest of the milk in a saucepan, but do not bring to the boil. Pour it over the egg mixture and whisk it well together.

6 Pour the milk mixture over the bread in the dish and allow to stand for about 30 minutes. Sprinkle the sugar on top of the pudding.

7 Stand the dish in a roasting pan and pour in sufficient hot water to come about halfway up the sides of the dish.

8 Bake at 180C/350F Gas mark 4, for about 45 minutes or until the pudding is well risen and the top is golden brown.

APPLE PIE

Hardware

sharp cook's medium-sized knife
pastry brush
rolling pin
250mm/10 inch pie plate

Ingredients

1 recipe of fruit pie pastry (page 75)
900g/2 lbs (2 lbs) cooking apples
150g/5 ozs (5 ozs) sugar
juice of one medium-sized juicy orange
a little milk to glaze

Method

1 Divide the pastry into two pieces, shape each into a flat ball, then roll out to cover the plate. Press one gently to fit the contour of the plate and trim off any surplus pastry. Press this into the other piece of pastry.

2 Peel the apples and slice them roughly on to the pastry lined plate, sprinkling sugar between the layers. (You will have quite a pile but don't worry). Pour the orange juice over the apples.

3 Roll out the remaining pastry so that it will just cover the apples and the edge of the plate. Dampen the edge of the base pastry, make 3 or 4 cuts in the lid pastry and position it to cover the apples.

4 Seal the edges, trim off any surplus pastry and press the edges to create an attractive appearance. Brush lightly with milk and sprinkle with sugar. Bake at 190C/375F Gas mark 5, for 45 to 50 minutes until pale golden brown.

Chef's Hints

In most domestic ovens it is difficult to bake the pastry thoroughly on the bottom, so follow the makers' suggestions if you do not know your oven very well. If the pie is going brown too quickly, reduce the heat by 6C/10F, and cover it loosely with foil, but do keep it in the oven for at least 45 minutes or the fruit will not be properly cooked.

Top Right: Sugar the sliced apples; Centre: Cover the apples with pastry; and Right: Trim off surplus pastry.

FRUIT PIE PASTRY

It will take 175g/6 ozs (6 ozs) of pastry to line a 250mm/10 inch plate, and a further 225g/8 ozs (8 ozs) to form a lid.

Hardware

medium-sized mixing bowl
small mixing bowl
palette knife
polythene
rolling pin
medium-sized knife

Ingredients

225g/8 ozs (8 ozs) plain flour (all purpose flour)
100g/4 ozs (4 ozs) margarine or butter
25g/1 oz (1 oz) lard (shortening)
1 × 2.5ml spoon/½ teaspoon (½ teaspoon) salt
1 medium-sized egg
1 × 15ml spoons/1 tablespoon (1 tablespoon) water

Method

1 All your ingredients for the pastry should be very cold, and it is better to make your pastry several hours in advance or even the day before, and keep it wrapped in the refrigerator until required. Allow it to return to nearly room temperature, before you roll it out.

2 Cut the margarine or butter and lard into 15mm/½ inch pieces and mix them through the flour with the salt.

3 Now rub the margarine or butter and lard into the flour until it is like fine breadcrumbs.

4 Whisk the egg and water together and mix into the flour and fat mixture, using a palette knife in a mixing and cutting procedure; they will eventually form a smooth block of pastry.

5 Tip the pastry on to a floured work surface, shape it into a flattened ball, wrap it in polythene and put into the refrigerator until required (for at least 1 hour).

Top Left: Press the edges together and seal them by crimping;
Centre: Brush the top lightly with milk;
Left: the baked Apple Pie.

IRISH SODA BREAD

Above: Cut the Soda Bread dough through to make four triangles and pull them slightly apart.

Hardware

large mixing bowl
jug
baking tray
medium saucepan

Ingredients

225g/8 ozs (8 ozs) plain flour (all purpose flour)
300ml/½ pint (1¼ cups) milk
225g/8 ozs (8 ozs) wheatmeal flour
1 × 5ml spoon/1 teaspoon (1 teaspoon) salt
1 × 5ml spoon/1 teaspoon (1 teaspoon) bicarbonate of soda (baking soda)
1 × 15ml spoon/1 tablespoon (1 tablespoon) cream of tartare
25g/1 oz (1 oz) butter
1 × 2.5ml spoon/½ teaspoon (½ teaspoon) sugar
a little extra milk if required

Method

1 Warm the milk very slightly until it is 23—24C/72-75F and whisk it to a smooth cream with the white flour. The resultant mixture should be 24C/75F, put it in a warm place also about 24C/75F to stand for 30 minutes. (This is known as a lactic ferment and the development of acid in this way is important to the finished character of the bread). If you can buy buttermilk, there is no need to do this — simply use the buttermilk instead of the lactic ferment. There is no need to warm it.

2 In a bowl mix all the dry ingredients (including the bicarbonate of soda and cream of tartare), together and rub in the butter, add the lactic ferment (or buttermilk) and mix lightly to a soft dough, adding the extra milk if required. The dough should not be stiff. Do not overmix this; it should take little effort and not much longer than one minute.

3 Sprinkle a little flour on to your work surface and drop the dough on to it. Shape into a ball.

4 Sprinkle flour on to a baking tray, drop the ball of dough on to it and press flat with your hands, until it is evenly round and about 30mm/1¼ inch thick.

5 Cut the dough right through, to make 4 triangles, pull them very slightly apart 3mm/⅛ inch. Dust the top with flour and bake 220C/425F Gas mark 7, for 30—35 minutes.

OLD FASHIONED HERB BREAD

This is a recipe I have developed from one used by my grandmother, passed down to her from her mother who was "in service" with a large Welsh family. It makes delightfully unusual bread with an open texture which is very light. You can vary the types of herbs used to your own liking, the ones suggested being my own favourites. I like to serve it with cheese or pâté or with cold meats. It is simplicity itself to make, requiring no kneading or shaping.

Hardware

Recommended baking tin (pan) sizes:
90mm/3½ inches × 65mm/2½ inches × 180mm/7 inches long = 450g/1 lb (1 lb)
100mm/4 inches wide × 90mm/3½ inches deep × 250mm/10 inches long = 900g/2 lbs (2 lbs)
large mixing bowl
medium-sized mixing bowl
wooden spoon
polythene

Ingredients

350g/12 ozs (12 ozs) strong flour
1 × 5ml spoon/1 teaspoon (1 teaspoon) salt
20g/¾ oz (¾ oz packet compressed) fresh yeast
300ml/½ pint (1¼ cups) milk
1 large egg
1 × 15ml spoon/1 tablespoon (1 tablespoon) oil
20g/¾ oz (¾ oz) sugar
1 × 5ml spoon/1 teaspoon (1 teaspoon) dried tarragon
sprinkling fennel seed

Method

1 Mix the egg and milk together in the large bowl and warm to blood heat.

2 Break the yeast down in this mixture, add the oil, sugar and tarragon, and mix together with a wooden spoon.

3 In the other bowl, mix the flour and salt together and sieve three quarters of it into the liquid ingredients, and beat well to produce an elastic creamy, batter-like dough. You should beat for 4—5 minutes or 3 minutes with an electric food mixer.

4 Mix in the remaining flour and scrape the mixture into a well-greased baking tin. The recipe is sufficient for two 450g/1 lb (1 lb) loaf tins or one 900g/2 lbs (2 lbs) tin.

5 Cover the tins with polythene, put in a warm place to rise for 35—40 minutes. Sprinkle the fennel seed on top of the loaves and bake at 180C/350F, Gas mark 4, for 25—30 minutes (35 minutes for a 900g/2 lbs (2 lbs) loaf.)

Left: Crusty Irish Soda Bread with cheese makes a delicious lunch or snack.

UNBELIEVABLY GOOD JAM TARTS

Hardware

large mixing bowl
small mixing bowl
fork
palette knife
patty tins
rolling pin
polythene

Ingredients (makes about 30)

175g/6 ozs (6 ozs) plain flour (all purpose flour)
150g/5 ozs (5 ozs) butter
1 medium-sized egg
225g/8 ozs (8 ozs) your favourite jam

Method

Pastry

1 All the ingredients must be very cold — straight from the refrigerator and kept cold whilst you are working.

2 Cut the butter into cubes (about 5mm/¼ inch). Sieve the flour into a bowl, rub in the butter gently with the fingertips and a knife until the mixture resembles fine breadcrumbs — be patient, the result is worthwhile.

3 Whisk the egg lightly with a fork and pour it into the flour mixture, mixing with a palette knife and using a mixing/cutting motion until the dough automatically goes together and forms a fairly smooth block of pastry. Stop mixing as soon as this happens and shape it by hand into a neat ball. Wrap it in polythene and put it into the refrigerator for 1 hour or until you need it.

Jam tarts

1 Take the pastry from the refrigerator and roll out with short light strokes until it is no more than 3mm/⅛ inch thick — thinner if possible.

2 Cut out circles the same size as your tins, and gently press the pastry into them. When you have used all your pastry (trimmings are carefully folded together and rolled out again) allow them to stand in a cold place for at least 1 hour.

3 In another bowl mix your favourite jam a little to break down any lumps and put about 1 x 5ml spoon/1 teaspoon (1 teaspoon) into each tart.

4 Bake at 190C/375F Gas mark 5, for 12—15 minutes. Do not let them get too brown as they will continue to cook a little after they have been taken out of the oven.

5 Leave the tarts in the tins for 5—10 minutes, then remove and put on a rack to cool.

A Very Fruity Cake

Jam Tarts ready for the oven.

A VERY FRUITY CAKE

Hardware

small knife
kitchen paper
medium-sized mixing bowl
large mixing bowl
bowl for eggs
sieve
wooden spoon
grater
metal skewer
200mm/ 8 inch cake tin or a long 900g/2 lbs (2 lbs) bread tin, lined with double layer of greaseproof (wax) paper.
(Obviously any shape of tin capable of holding the cake mix is satisfactory).
tin foil

Ingredients

100g/4 ozs (4 ozs) glacé (candied) pineapple
100g/4 ozs (4 ozs) glacé (candied) cherries
75g/3 ozs (3 ozs) stem (preserved) stem ginger
50g/2 ozs (2 ozs) mixed glacé (candied) peel
100g/4 ozs (4 ozs) dried apricots
350g/12 ozs (12 ozs) sultanas (seedless white raisins)
50g/2 ozs (2 ozs) walnuts, roughly chopped
50g/2 ozs (2 ozs) brazil nuts, broken in half
225g/8 ozs (8 ozs) butter
225g/8 ozs (8 ozs) caster sugar (granulated sugar)
50g/2 ozs (2 ozs) ground almonds
4 large eggs
225g/8 ozs (8 ozs) plain flour (all purpose flour)
grated rind of 1 orange and 1 lemon
juice of 1 orange
6 drops vanilla essence (vanilla extract)
3 drops almond essence (almond extract)
1 good measure brandy (optional)

Method

1 Cut the pineapple, ginger and apricots into roughly 15mm/½ inch pieces and wash the syrup or sugar off them and the glacé cherries; leave to dry on kitchen paper overnight.

2 Put the sultanas to soak in hot water for 10 minutes. Drain off the water and leave them to dry on kitchen paper overnight.

3 Place all the fruit, candied peel, broken nuts and half the ground almonds into a bowl and mix them together.

4 Put the sugar into the large mixing bowl, and add the butter cut into small pieces. I like to leave the bowl in a warm place for 15 minutes or so until the butter is soft (do not let it get oily).

5 To the sugar and butter mixture, add the grated orange and lemon rind, the almond and vanilla essence and beat well until the mixture is light and creamy (about 5 minutes).

6 Mix in the remaining ground almonds and approximately a quarter (50g/2 ozs (2 ozs)) of the flour.

7 Beat the eggs (which should be at room temperature) together and add them in six successive equal quantities, beating well between each addition.

8 Sieve the flour into the mixture and fold it in. When it is nearly incorporated, add the fruit and nut mixture and the orange juice. Mix this in until it is evenly distributed throughout the mixture. Empty into the cake tin, lined with a double layer of greaseproof paper, and bake for 2¼ hours at 170C/325F Gas mark 3. You can test if it is ready by piercing it with a metal skewer. If it comes out clean, the cake is done. If you feel it is getting too brown during baking, cover loosely with foil.

9 Leave the cake on a wire rack to cool. Whilst the cake is still warm, pierce it deeply with a metal skewer in several places and then pour on the brandy. Wrap it loosely in foil and leave the brandy to permeate the cake.

SANDRA'S CHEESECAKE

Hardware

2 × 180mm/7 inch cake tins with loose bottoms
polythene bag
rolling pin
mixing bowl
wooden spoon
small saucepan

Ingredients (serves 8)

Base mixture
225g/8 ozs (8 ozs) digestive biscuits (Graham crackers)
75g/3 ozs (3 ozs) butter

Topping
225g/8 ozs (8 ozs) cream cheese
225g/8 ozs (8 ozs) Philadelphia cheese
4 medium-sized eggs
225g/8 ozs (8 ozs) caster sugar (granulated sugar)
450ml/¾ pint (2 cups) soured (cultured) cream
2 × 15ml/2 tablespoons (2 tablespoons) sugar

Below: Chiffon Cheesecake with Black Cherry topping.

Sandra's Cheesecake

Method

1 Put the biscuit into the polythene bag, tie the top and crush with the rolling pin; tip into bowl.

2 Melt the butter in a saucepan and pour it into the bowl.

3 Grease the cake tins and divide the biscuit mixture equally between the two. Press down firmly to form the base of the cheesecake.

4 Bake the bases for about 5 mintutes in a 190C/375F Gas mark 5 oven, and allow to cool.

5 Mix the cheeses and the caster sugar in the bowl. Make sure they are well blended. The amount of sugar may be varied according to your personal taste.

6 Add the eggs one at a time, beating very well between each.

7 Pour the cheese mixture into the two tins and bake for 30 minutes at 190C/375F Gas mark 5.

8 Remove the cakes from the oven. Turn the oven up to 200C/400F, Gas mark 6. Mix the soured cream with the two tablespoons of sugar.

9 Pour the soured cream topping over the two cakes and bakc for a further 3—5 minutes.

10 Allow to cool before removing from the tins. always make two of these at once because they are a great favourite; if one is left, it makes a nice present!

CHIFFON CHEESECAKE

The bowl and whisk must be spotlessly clean when making this cheesecake. To separate an egg — have two bowls ready. Crack an egg as near in half as you can; hold the egg over one bowl, carefully pull the shell apart and pour out the white of the egg into the bowl. Tipping the yolk from one half of the shell into the other, pour all the white out and then tip the yolk into the second bowl. This method will take some practice; alternatively, you can buy yourself an 'egg separator'.

Hardware

rolling pin
small container for gelatine (gelatin)
1 × 15ml spoon/1 tablespoon (1 tablespoon)
bowl for whisking (beating) egg white
whisk
1 large bowl
wooden spoon
1 small saucepan
180-200mm/7-8 inch loose-bottomed cake tin
1 medium-sized bowl

Ingredients (serves 4)

biscuit base

100g/4 ozs (4 ozs) digestive biscuits (Graham crackers)
1 × 5ml spoon/1 teaspoon (1 teaspoon) ground cinnamon
50g/2 ozs (2 ozs) butter

filling

1 × 15ml spoon/1 tablespoon (1 tablespoon) hot water
7g/¼ oz (1 envelope) gelatine (gelatin)
225g/8 ozs (8 ozs) low fat cream cheese
75g/3 ozs (3 ozs) caster sugar (granulated sugar)
150ml/¼ pint (⅔ cup) double cream (heavy cream)
2 medium-sized eggs
juice of one lemon
50g/2 ozs (2 ozs) sultanas (seedless white raisins)
50g/2 ozs (2 ozs) glacé (candied) cherries, halved

Method

1 Crumble the biscuits into fine crumbs (by putting the biscuits into a plastic bag or between two sheets of paper and crushing with the rolling pin). Put the crumbs into a bowl and mix in the cinnamon. Melt the butter in a saucepan and mix it into the crumbs. Spread the mixture evenly over the bottom of the tin and bake for 6 minutes at 200C/400F Gas mark 6. Allow to cool.

2 Melt the gelatine in the hot water and allow to cool.

3 Meanwhile, in a bowl mix the cheese, cream, sugar and lemon juice together.

4 Separate the whites from the eggs and mix the yolks into the cheese mixture.

5 Mix the gelatine into the cheese mixture.

6 Whisk the egg whites in a bowl until stiff and fold them carefully into the cheese mixture. Fold in the cherries and sultanas.

7 Pour the mixture on top of the biscuit base. Refrigerate overnight before removing from the tin, and add the topping of your choice.

Chef's Hints

The fruit can be replaced with any glacé (candied) fruit, but ensure that it is fresh and tender.

This cheesecake can be made with any of the ready-made toppings available in cans from supermarkets. Leave out the sultanas (seedless white raisins) and cherries, of course!

Variations on this are:

Marmalade Chiffon Cheesecake
Leave out the sultanas (seedless white raisins) and cherries. Spread the biscuit base with 100g/4 ozs (4 ozs) of your favourite chunky marmalade. Put the cheese mixture on top and refrigerate as normal.

Mandarin Chiffon Dessert
Drain the juice from a small can of mandarin oranges. Spread the segments over the biscuit base and spread the mixture on top. Refrigerate as for above, and omit the cherries and sultanas (seedles white raisins) again.

TOASTED SANDWICHES

What a simple, quick and delicious snack this is! Virtually any bread can be used, but, for simplicity, try the ready-sliced variety, medium in thickness, or special toasting bread. Brown breads of most types also make delicious toast.

A toasted sandwich is exactly as the name suggests and is made by lightly buttering slices of bread, putting on a filling of your choice, placing the top layer and then toasting. Obviously you cannot use a toaster — unless you have the specially devised 'Toastreet' machine. The sandwiches should be toasted under a grill. It is important to toast slowly, so that the sandwich heats through.

Suggested Fillings

1 Cooked ham with grated cheese (or try smoked cheese instead).

2 Grated Cheddar cheese and grated apple.

3 Tenderly cooked steak, finely shredded, with fried onions and French mustard or ketchup.

4 Crispy grilled bacon with a mixture of cream cheese and sultanas.

5 Corned beef broken up and mixed with your favourite chutney.

6 Cooked chicken, mixed with white sauce (see Chicken and Ham Pie, page 66) and sweetcorn (don't use too much sauce).

Never make the filling too wet, and judge the amount for the filling according to the number of sandwiches you are making.

Toasted Open Sandwiches

For these, use muffins, baps or barm cakes; split them and toast them very lightly on both sides. Butter the cut side. Toppings suitable for these are numbers 1,2 and 4 (above) but with 1 and 2 let the cheese be on top, and with 4 only lightly cook the bacon.

The following recipe makes a good spread to use for one of these sandwiches. It is really good on a wholemeal (wholewheat) bap.

Ingredients (sufficient for 4 halved baps)

225g/8 ozs (8 ozs) Cheddar cheese, grated
2 × 5ml spoons/2 teaspoons (2 teaspoons) French mustard
1 clove garlic, finely chopped
pinch nutmeg
2 × 5ml spoons/2 teaspoons (2 teaspoons) Worcestershire sauce
2 × 15ml spoons/2 tablespoons (2 tablespoons) double cream (heavy cream)
1 × 5ml spoon/1 teaspoon (1 teaspoon) lemon juice
pinch salt

Simply mix all these ingredients together, spread over the toasted bap, then grill until the topping is golden and bubbling (for about 5 minutes).

Fried Bread

Very fattening, and bad for the arteries no doubt, but delicious with poached eggs! You need to have the oil in the frying pan (skillet) nearly 15mm/½ inch deep.

Trim the crusts from medium-thick slices of bread. Heat the oil until a crumb of bread sizzles on contact, then slip in the slices and fry them on each side until a pale golden brown. Drain well on absorbent paper and serve with a poached egg. So much better than toast! Children love this with jam, ketchup or marmalade.

PAIN PERDUE

Not good for a health fanatic, but cheap and simple to make, and great to eat.

Hardware

whisk
flat dish (for soaking the bread)
absorbent paper
knife
frying pan (skillet)
small saucepan

Ingredients (serves 6)

Syrup
100g/4 ozs (4 ozs) caster sugar (granulated sugar)
150ml/¼ pint (⅔ cup) water
50mm/2 inches of thinly pared lemon rind
pinch cinnamon
120ml/4 fl.ozs (½ cup) sherry

Bread
1 medium-sized egg
150ml/¼ pint (⅔ cup) milk
6 thick slices of white bread (preferably stale)
cooking oil

Method

Syrup
Simmer all the ingredients (except the sherry) together in a saucepan for 10 minutes. Allow to cool, and then add the sherry.

Bread
1 Whisk the egg and milk together in the flat dish.

2 Trim the crusts from the bread and dip the slices into the egg and milk. Allow them to absorb the mixture until there is no free liquid.

3 Fry the slices in good quality oil until golden and crisp. Drain well on absorbent paper. Serve with the sugar syrup.

PAIN BAGNA

Hardware

sharp knife

Ingredients (serves 2)

1 French stick of bread
1 clove garlic
6 black (ripe) olives, stoned (pitted)
6 green olives, stoned (pitted)
1 red or green pepper, sliced
4 firm medium-sized tomatoes, sliced
anchovies or sardines (optional)
2 × 15ml spoons/2 tablespoons (2 tablespoons) olive oil
2 × 5ml spoons/2 teaspoons (2 teaspoons) wine vinegar
1 small onion, sliced

Method

1 Cut the stick of bread in half, through the length.

2 Finely chop a clove of garlic and sprinkle it over one cut surface; spread the surface with the stoned olives, anchovies or sardines, pieces of pepper, tomato, and onion. Afterwards pour olive oil and wine vinegar over this salad.

3 Put the top half of the roll back in position and press the sandwich together. You can put a heavy weight over the filled roll for a few minutes to bind it.

4 Cut the filled bread into 4 equal lengths (and serve with a bottle of red wine!).

Chef's Hints

Suggestions for other additions: cheeses, chicory (Belgian endive), celery, lettuce, French beans, (cooked and cold, or raw), cold potato, smoked ham, relishes and cooked chicken.

SALADS

Basic green salads

Lettuce, chicory (Belgian endive), curly endive, green pepper, celery, young dandelion leaves, watercress. All these can be used in a green salad. There are other more obscure salad vegetables, but these are easily available and when fresh and crisp are quite delicious. Do ensure that anything used is spotlessly clean. (I like to wash salads in cold water to which I have added a teaspoon or so of sugar). Do not use any parts which are limp or discoloured.

Always present them in a large bowl, or individual bowls, so that when the salad is dressed — at the last moment — it can be tossed and turned with abandon, without fear of decorating your fellow diners with pieces of greenery or oily dressing!

I am not very fond of mixed salads, as there is always something that someone doesn't like and certain ingredients tend to respond better to different dressings. I like, therefore, to serve a choice of several salads so that people can please themselves, each salad vegetable having its most suitable dressing and the individual flavours being more easily recognised and enjoyed.

The following is a small but interesting selection to add variety to any meal.

Cucumber Salad

It is simple and good to slice cucumbers, sprinkle them with a little sugar and vinegar and serve them. But, it is so much better if you go to a little more trouble. There is no need to cut off the green skin, unless you violently object to it; score with a fork by all means, to give that attractive serrated effect, but I simply slice it very thinly, slightly at an angle to give oval shapes. Put these on a plate and sprinkle them liberally with salt. Leave them in the fridge for at least one hour. Tip them into a large sieve and wash them well to get rid of the salt, then allow to drain on kitchen paper. Spread them in a flat bowl, sprinkle with very little sugar and white wine vinegar, chill and serve. This treatment seems to lift that fresh cucumber flavour and gives them a very delicate texture.

Tomato Salad

This salad is good only with top quality tomatoes. The best are Marmonde or perhaps

some good firm English tomatoes, but straight from the greenhouse. Cut them into thin slices, sprinkle lightly with a little sugar, then dress with a basic French Dressing. Allow them to marinate for at least 1 hour in your refrigerator.

Mushroom Salad
Buy clean fresh firm button mushrooms, trim the stalks, wipe them clean and then slice very thinly — dress with Sour Cream Dressing.

Apple and Walnut Salad
Peel and dice a firm, sharp eating apple and cut 2 or 3 white stalks of celery into 5mm/¼ inch slices. Mix them together, add about a dozen chopped shelled walnuts, and dress with a Sour Cream Dressing.

Cole Slaw
Very, very finely shred a firm white cabbage, some onion and sweet firm apples. If you have a very coarse grater, it is possible to do it on that. The proportions should be 4 parts cabbage, 1 part apple, and ½ part onion. You can also add a little grated carrot if you wish. Mix them well together and dress liberally with Sour Cream Dressing, or basic French Dressing. Allow to marinate for 1 hour or more before use.

FRENCH DRESSING

Salad dressings are very much a matter of personal taste. Once you have an indication of basic requirements, the varieties you can evolve are many. For me, most dressings contain too much vinegar and I like to use at least 4 parts of oil to 1 part of vinegar.

Ingredients

4 x 15ml spoons/4 tablespoons (¼ cup) olive oil
1 x 15ml spoon/1 tablespoon (1 tablespoon) white wine vinegar
1 x 2.5ml spoon/½ teaspoon (½ teaspoon) sugar

Method

Dissolve the sugar in the vinegar, then whisk (beat) in the oil with a fork. If the oil and vinegar are similar temperatures and you whisk (beat) hard enough, you will form an emulsion — not very stable, but it will hold long enough to dress your salad and, if it does separate, it will be easy enough to whisk (beat) together again.

Simple variations are made by using different oils, although for me there is nothing as good as olive oil, in any of its various qualities. Vinegars are different; malt vinegar, or the white vinegar you can buy, should never be used in salad dressing. Always use a red or white wine vinegar. For variety, use a flavoured vinegar — tarragon is my favourite, but there are many others. Also you can try cider vinegar or sherry vinegar.

To give further variety to your basic dressing, try whisking (beating) in a little mustard, French or English, or even a little tomato ketchup.

SOUR CREAM DRESSING

Ingredients

3 x 15ml spoons/3 tablespoons (3 tablespoons) olive oil
2 x 15ml spoons/2 tablespoons (2 tablespoons) single cream (light cream)
1 x 15ml spoon/1 tablespoon (1 tablespoon) lemon juice
1 x 5ml spoon/1 teaspoon (1 teaspoon) sugar

Method

Mix all the above well together; then, if you like, season it lightly with white pepper and a little salt. You may also like to add a teaspoon or so of Dijon mustard.

CHEESE WITH YOUR MEAL

Napoleon Bonaparte was never one of my favourite historical characters, until I discovered what a service he did for the world in connection with cheese. At some time during his wanderings around Europe, he stopped off at a remote Normandy inn where he first tasted the delights of Camembert.

History records that Napoleon was so delighted with the cheese that he kissed the maid who served him, helped himself to further generous portions and no doubt, to coin a famous phrase, murmured something like 'not just *now,* Josephine.'

Certainly, the lovers of French cheese lay the credit for Camembert's success entirely at Napoleon's larder door and I am the last person to wish to upset the gastronomic entente cordiale. Although I have no idea exactly what else Napoleon had to eat on that historic occasion, I hope he regarded cheese as I do...something which should be served *after* the main course and *before* the dessert.

Cheese, as part of a meal, is something that can be lingered over and which allows you to relax after the main course. You can enjoy finishing what remains of the wine and prepare your palate for what should be the crowning glory of every meal...the dessert. Believe me, you will not only enjoy the dessert all the more after the cheese, but also look forward to it with enthusiasm.

To appreciate **Blue Stilton** at its best, it should be a creamy white, marbled with blue, and turning a delicate amber towards the thin brown outside crust. Experience has taught me to avoid a Blue Stilton which is more than 5mm/¼ inch thick at the crust. As for those infidels who soak this noble cheese with port wine, or who scoop it from the middle with a spoon, they can only do their stomachs a great dis-service. Anybody really wishing to appreciate the full range of flavours which the Blue Stilton provides should always slice it across the surface from crust to centre.

Lancashire, Cheshire and Wensleydale are three of the better-known English cheeses and are available in different strengths. I use all three frequently for snacks, ploughman's lunches and in cooking, but Lancashire is my favourite for tasting and for fondue.

Cheddar, Double Gloucester and Red Leicester are also good for cooking and for snacks. They grate well and are delicious toasted, on top of pizzas, or sprinkled on pastas and in soups. Whenever I serve minestrone, for instance, I do not just sprinkle one of these cheeses on top, but I also stir some into the soup. In my recipes for cheese sauces, you will notice that I recommend the Cheddar or the Double Gloucester, because I regard the Red Leicester as rather too colourful for that purpose.

Caboc is a soft, buttery, Scottish cheese, which is coated on the outside with oatmeal. Perhaps it is not as widely enjoyed as it deserves to be. It is more like a cheesey butter with a mild flavour, which tastes delicious on dry biscuits or on oatcakes.

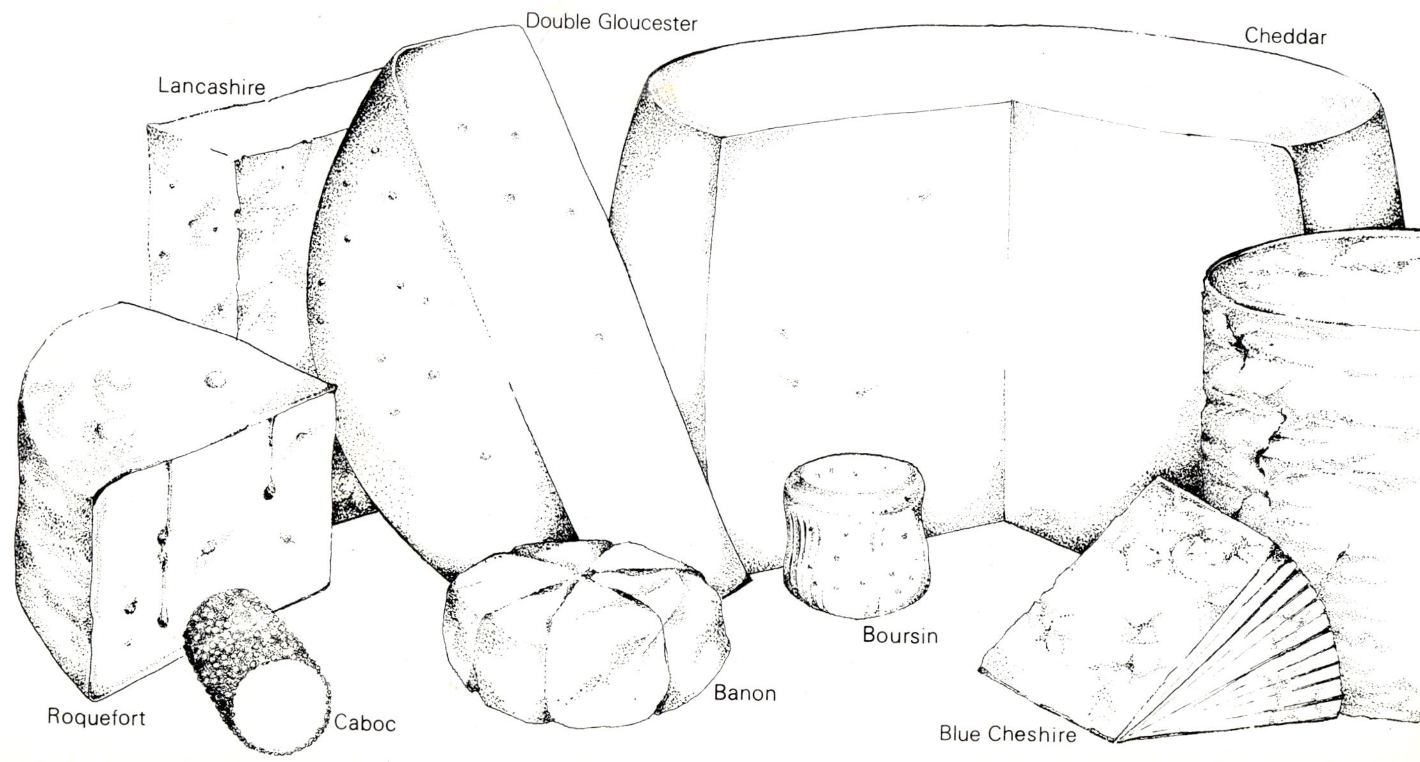

Roquefort is rightly regarded by French gourmets with the same appreciation that a British trencherman has for the Blue Stilton. The cheeses have a lot in common. A similar strain of mould is used, but the milk processing and the different climates, produce two cheeses which are wonderfully different.

Roquefort is made from ewes' milk and the curds are innoculated with penicillium Roqueforti. The curds are then placed in the famous caves in Causses, in Aquitaine, in such unique conditions that this cheese cannot be produced anywhere else in the world.

Both Roquefort and Blue Stilton are delicious crumbled into salad dressings, on sandwiches, or when blended with butter and spread on top of grilled steak.

Brie is another deservedly popular cheese, which can be enjoyed at various stages of its maturity. It should have a thin white rind, which is also delicious. Brie is at its best when the rind is starting to bulge and the cheese is becoming 'runny', although the rind should never be discoloured, or the cheese excessively 'runny'. Its creamy, mushroomy taste can also be a little fruity.

Camembert is also at its best when it starts to 'run'. Neither Camembert nor Brie, however, should be allowed to become too ripe, otherwise the flavour and smell become cloyingly strong.

Goat cheeses have been popular in France for a very long time, but it is only comparatively recently that they have made their appearance elsewhere. Although they are normally small in size and vary in texture and flavour, they are well worth sampling for those of us who like a strong cheese.

Banon is one goat cheese to which I am particularly partial. It is made in 25mm/1 inch thick discs, weighing about 100g/4 ozs (4 ozs). It has a pleasant nutty taste and is wrapped in leaves.

Cabecou is a cheese which takes its name from a word which means 'little goat'. The cheeses are also little, no larger than 40mm/1½ inches in diameter with a greyish blue rind and a unique milky flavour.

Grape Cheese, 'Tomme au Raisin', is a processed cheese which I find particularly pleasant. It is coated with toasted grape pips which give it the flavour of the grape.

Boursin consists of a range of commercially manufactured cheeses, but I do not hesitate to recommend them to anybody. There are many delightful flavours, which range from natural and garlic to herbs and peppercorn. Try blending the natural Boursin with sugar and whisked egg whites, serve with fresh raspberries and you have a mouthwatering dessert, Fromage à la Crème.

Parmesan is the grated white cheese which we all sprinkle over pasta dishes, Minestrone (page 34) and Lasagne (page 53). However, to really appreciate the true Parmesan flavour, you need to buy it whole and grate it as you require it. That is when you spot the difference between the real cheese and the commercial Parmesan sold in containers.

It is worth remembering, also, that cheese is one of the world's most complete and versatile foods, which has virtually no waste. It has been around for a long time, though much as I adore cheese I am not too sure that I would care to have emulated the ancient Persian philosopher Zoroaster. Apparently, for some 20 years, his diet consisted of nothing but cheese. If you reckon Zoroaster needed something like 454g/1 lb (1 lb) a day, then he must have munched through almost 3,314 kilos (almost 7,300 pounds) altogether. And that really does take some swallowing!

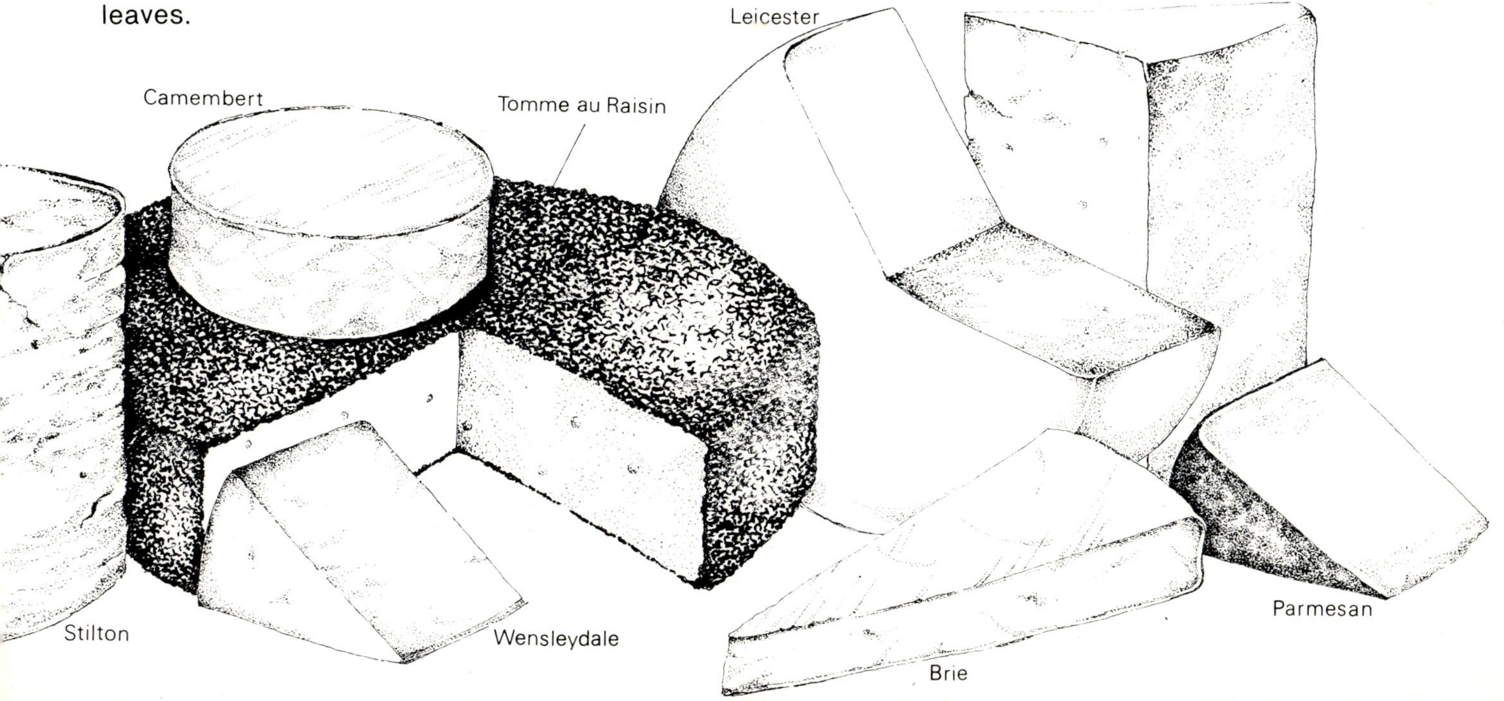

DRINKS WITH YOUR MEAL

It is easy to ridicule the professional wine taster as he goes about his tasks and many pleasures...surrounded as he is by bottles, spittoons, delicately-shaped glasses and plates of biscuits, in a room which rings with the sounds of strange adjectives! Yet we have to rely upon those people with exceptional palates to discover and recommend to shippers and wholesale buyers the wines which eventually reach our tables. In fact, most people, after a few years of serious wine drinking, acquire a basic knowledge of their favourites and why they prefer them. The same can be said for aperitifs. Marketing skills alone are not responsible for our liking to a particular sherry, for example, it is simply that we learn as we drink.

We should therefore try to observe the ground rules of wine-manship, by learning as much as we can about wines which we drink with our food. After all, the rules have become established after centuries of drinking, discussion and, more recently, scientific investigation.

I appreciate that the very basic guide-lines may not suit everybody's palate, because there are people who drink only white wines and those who drink only red. But the white wine will not taste as good with red meat, and a red wine is not at its best with fish. Certain wines bring out the best flavours in certain foods and most wines complement the foods with which it is recommended they should be served.

Basically the rules about wines are simple.

1. Always drink dry wine before sweet wine. Otherwise, the dry wine will make the sweet wine taste sour. Sweet wines are, sometimes, served with a fish course, but when that occurs I always advise a dish in between, to clear your palate in readiness for the drier wines to follow.
2. Always take light wines before heavy wines. A full-rounded, heavy wine will otherwise make any light wine which follows appear quite tasteless.
3. Red wines with fish may make the fish taste sulphurous.
4. White wines with red meats are more palatable, but they do not bring out the best flavours in food.
5. Never serve dry wines with sweet food.

WINE WITH FOOD

Whenever I buy wine, I like to feel that my selection is one that is all it claims to be. By that, I mean that it honestly reflects its origins by (a) being bottled in the country in which it was made and (b) that it carries the stamp of approval by the appropriate authority.

The official stamps of approval are not hard to remember. The good French wines should display the initials A.C., which stand for Appellation Controlée. In Italy, wines of quality should be stamped with D.O.C., which is the Denominization di Origine Controllata.

Unfortunately, we cannot always afford the wines which we would really enjoy most of all, so it makes a lot of sense to find out which of the cheaper wines appeal to our palates. This is even more a matter of personal taste and although the French 'vins du pays' do not please *my* palate, I can enjoy the inexpensive and widely available full red Corrida or the Hirondelle wines. There is also an excellent range of inexpensive German wines like Moselblumchen, Liebfraumilch, Piesporter and Bernkastellar. The better quality German labels can be spotted by phrases like Qualitatswein, Qualitatswein mit Pradiktat or Kabinett Spätlese, Auslese, Beerenauslese, etc.

APERITIFS

Served before a meal, aperitifs certainly sharpen the appetite for the good food that should follow. But there is certainly no reason why we should stick to the usual gins-and-something, or Scotches-and-something-else. Dry to medium sherries, or a dry Madeira, served slightly chilled, are hard to beat as aperitifs to encourage the appetite.

Sparkling wines are also stimulating aperitifs, but these need not be champagnes. You can always try the German Sekt, or Kriter, or Veuve du Vernay — and I much prefer the dry wines in these cases.

Other aperitifs which many people enjoy are Pernod (served with water, orange juice or tonic water), and Campari and its recommended mixtures (try it with chilled orange juice). An aperitif which is quite different from most others is Crème de Cassis — a blackcurrant liqueur — mixed with chilled white wine and ice.

Vermouth is probably one of the world's most popular aperitifs, and there is a very wide selection. Try some of the more unusual Vermouths. Apart from Noilly Prat, Martini and Cinzano, there is the bitter-sweet Italian Punt à Mes and the French Vermouth Chambery, which has a truly unique herbal aroma.

WHITE WINES

Frankly, I canot really avoid repeating that the best way to enjoy wines is to match your wines to the food. With white wines, that means serving them with fish or white meat. In this category, I never hesitate to recommend the wines which come from the Loire, Muscadet, Touraine, Sancerre and Vouvray regions. Montrachet, of course, is regarded as the very best of dry white wines and Bordeaux is rightly regarded as the best region for sweet white wines. The Sauternes and Barsacs I prefer as dessert wines, to serve after a meal.

RED WINES

There is really an almost bewildering range of red wines and my advice is to stick to the rules I have already stated. Select those which are bottled in the country of origin, learn something about vintages and some basic knowledge of the language is very useful when reading the labels.

A red burgundy, or claret, goes well with roast meats, though I would prefer burgundy to claret with highly-spiced dishes. Of course, wines are often selected on the basis of their price. The French wines which make financial sense are those from the Beaujolais Villages like Brouilly, Fleurie, Julienas, Moulin à Vent and St Amour.

Probably the most prominent range of Italian wines includes Torgiano Rubescu, Montepulchino, Brunello, Barolo, Valpolicella Clasico and Chianti Classico — all excellent value for your money.

It really is becoming difficult to keep up with the vast range of Spanish wines that are appearing on the market. Fortunately, they are almost always reasonably inexpensive and very seldom undrinkable. Among those I enjoy are Marques de Riscal, Marques de Murrieta and almost any wine from the Rioja region.

May Bacchus help to please *your* palate!

COOKERY TERMS UNSCRAMBLED

Aïoli: Garlic mayonnaise, often served with fish.

Americaine: French term indicating the use of tomato in the preparation of meat, fish, vegetables and egg dishes.

Bain-marie: Saucepan placed in larger pan of simmering water; often used to prepare sauces, creams, etc., which need to be cooked over indirect heat.

Baste: Pouring juices from the pan over meat, fish, etc., to keep it moist during cooking.

Béchamel: Basic white sauce; cheese, cream or eggs can be added for flavour.

Beurre manié: Butter thickened with flour; used for sauces.

Bind: Thicken with breadcrumbs, cream, eggs, flour or stock; or hold together ingredients with eggs, fat or sauces.

Blanch: Scald or whiten by putting into boiling water.

Blend: Mix gently, to achieve even consistency.

Braise: Process of browning meat, fish or vegetables, over high heat to preserve juices and then simmering (covered) for long cooking periods in small amounts of liquid.

Casserole: Ovenproof dish (usually made of metal, glass or earthenware) with tightly-fitting lid, used for cooking as well as serving; also refers to the food prepared in such a way.

Chine: Remove the bone that joins chops together (see Loin of Lamb with Herbs, page 40).

Clarify: Process by which liquids (butter, dripping, soups, jellies, etc.) are made clear by filtering, to remove sediments.

Consommé: Stock (bouillon) that has been reduced to intensify its flavour, and then clarified.

Coddle: Cook in a tightly covered dish, which is removed from heat after the contents reach boiling point.

Cream: Using a heavy spoon or spatula, combine sugar and fat, for the first stage in cake-making.

Croûtons: Small cubes of bread fried in butter or oil, and served in soups as a garnish.

Curdle: Coagulation (as in scrambled eggs), which can be accidental (milk, sauces, etc.).

Cut in: Combine fat with selected ingredients by cutting downwards with a knife continuously until the fat has become finely flaked.

Daube: Way of cooking meat, similar to braising.

Deep fat: Hot oil or fat which covers food as it fries.

Dice: Cut into small cubes.

Entrée: Traditionally, the dish served between fish and meat course. In America, it is usually the first course.

Flake: Breaking into individual pieces — as with fish, or grating into slices — as with cheese or chocolate.

Flambé: Means 'flamed' in French. Warm alcohol, pour on dish, and set alight.

Fold in: Blend a light mixture (flour or egg whites) gently into another mixture.

Fool: Cold mixture of fruit purée and whipped cream.

Fritters: Food covered in batter, which is then shallow or deep fried.

Game: Deer, grouse, hare, partridge, pheasant, pigeon, ptarmigan, quail, rabbit, etc.

Garnish: Decoration (edible) of a finished dish to improve its appearance.

Giblets: Edible innards of poultry and game, generally reserved for making stock (bouillon) or gravy.

Glacé: Candied, frozen, glazed or iced.

Glaze: Glossy surface on meats or pastries, by

coating with beaten egg, jam, jelly, milk, sugar or syrup.

Griddle: Flat metal plate for cooking scones and cakes.

Hamburger: Originally the German word for a minced beef patty.

Hors d'oeuvre: French for a selection of food, generally served as a starter.

Hot pot: English stew, with potatoes on top and cooked slowly.

Infuse: Extract flavour by steeping in liquid (sometimes boiling, as with tea).

Knead: Working dough (batter) until all the ingredients are combined to the required elasticity; especially important in bread-making.

Larding: Threading strip of pork fat with a larding needle into lean meat, to make it moist and contribute flavour during cooking.

Marinade: Seasoned liquid, cooked or not, in which food is submerged, for it to gain flavours and soften.

Marmite: Cooking pot of metal or earthenware, with a lid. (It has given its name to certain soups and commercial yeast extracts).

Medaillion: Round slice.

Meunière (à la): Way of preparing fish, in which it is rolled in flour, fried in butter, and garnished with lemon juice and chopped parsley.

Mornay: Cheese sauce, often served with eggs, vegetables or fish.

Mousse: Smooth light mixture, made with egg whites, cream and generally gelatine (gelatin). Served hot or cold.

Parboiling: Partly boil, and drain; then continue cooking in another way.

Pare: Shave or cut (as with lemon rind from the fruit).

Pasta: Dried flour paste, which is available in many shapes and sizes (see pages 52—55).

Pâtisserie: Pastries; the art of the pastry cook; a pastry shop.

Pizza: Italian word for the traditional open savoury pie (see pages 62—63).

Poach: Cook in a liquid in an open pan, just below boiling point.

Pot roast: Meat cooked slowly in a lidded pot with a little liquid and flavoured ingredients.

Prove: Allow prepared dough (batter) to rise, before it is cooked.

Purée: French word for the creamy smooth texture created by liquidising (blending), sieving or pounding in a mortar.

Ragoût: French word for a slowly-cooked brown stew.

Reduce: Boil a liquid mixture (such as a sauce, gravy or soup) in an uncovered pan, so that some of it evaporates, leaving the remainder thickened and with its flavour intensified.

Render: Melt down fat gently in the oven and then strain, or boil with a little water in an uncovered pan and strain when it clears.

Sauté: French term for quick frying in a shallow pan, using only a little fat.

Scald: Plunge food (tomatoes, peaches, plums, etc.) into boiling water for a few seconds to make peeling easy; or to heat a liquid (milk for example) to just under boiling point.

Sear: Seal juices in (generally) meat by frying over a fierce heat for a short time.

Seasoning: Word for flavourings such as salt, pepper, herbs and spices.

Simmer: Cook in liquid just below boiling point, when bubbles occasionally break the surface.

Skim: Remove impurities from surfaces of sauces, soups, stocks (bouillons), etc.

Steam: Cook in a moist heat.

Stew: Cook slowly at simmering point in an enclosed saucepan. Suited to coarse-fibred meats.

Stock: (American — bouillon). Liquid in which meat and bones have been cooked with herbs and other bases, and then strained.

Whisk: (American — beat). Add air to a mixture by hand.

Zest: Rind of citrus fruit, without the white membrane which connects it to the fruit.

INDEX

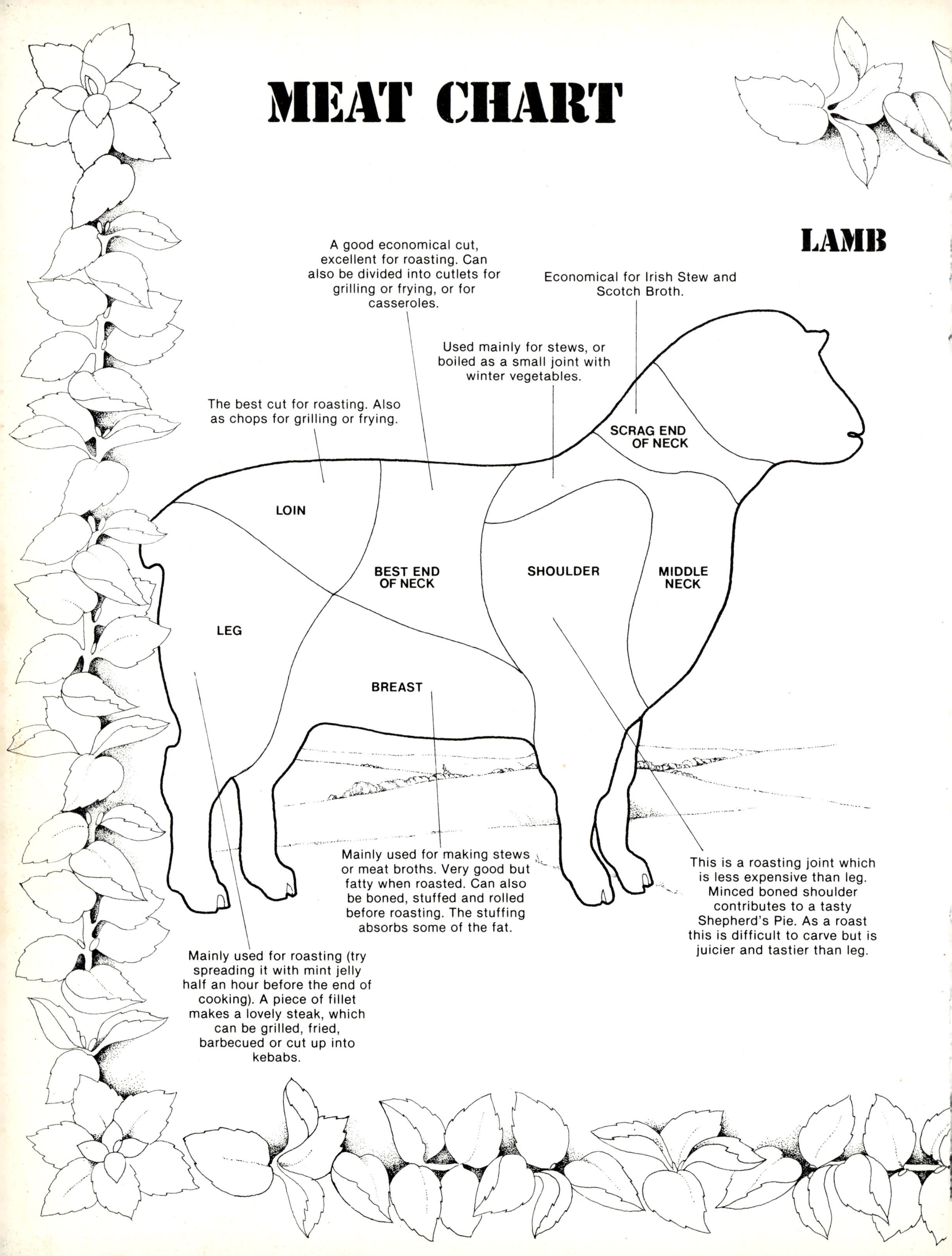
MEAT CHART
LAMB
A good economical cut, excellent for roasting. Can also be divided into cutlets for grilling or frying, or for casseroles.
Economical for Irish Stew and Scotch Broth.
Used mainly for stews, or boiled as a small joint with winter vegetables.
The best cut for roasting. Also as chops for grilling or frying.
SCRAG END OF NECK
LOIN
BEST END OF NECK
SHOULDER
MIDDLE NECK
LEG
BREAST
Mainly used for making stews or meat broths. Very good but fatty when roasted. Can also be boned, stuffed and rolled before roasting. The stuffing absorbs some of the fat.
This is a roasting joint which is less expensive than leg. Minced boned shoulder contributes to a tasty Shepherd's Pie. As a roast this is difficult to carve but is juicier and tastier than leg.
Mainly used for roasting (try spreading it with mint jelly half an hour before the end of cooking). A piece of fillet makes a lovely steak, which can be grilled, fried, barbecued or cut up into kebabs.